ASVAB

CRAM

Ace the ASVAB with One Week of Test Prep And Free Online Practice Tests 2021 / 2022 Study Guide

By Steve Weber

Published by Stephen W. Weber
Printed in the United States of America
Weber Books www.WeberBooks.com
ISBN: 978-1-936560-08-0

Your purchase of this book provides unlimited access to online ASVAB practice tests. Test yourself using the same format and time limits as the computerized ASVAB.

Go to: www.ASVABcram.com

Contents

▶ MY TAKE ON THE ASVAB

One Friday, midway through my senior year of high school, an Air Force recruiter showed up at my school. Word spread quickly about his irresistible proposition: spend the afternoon with him, and he would get permission for us to skip the whole afternoon of classes. And, perhaps the best part—he'd buy our lunch at a local seafood joint. All we had to do was go to his office after lunch and take a test—the ASVAB. It sounded like a great deal to me and my best friend, Mason, and a dozen of our classmates.

Until then, I hadn't thought much about joining the service. I hadn't thought much about college, either. In fact, I had no plan whatsoever for a career after school. So, even though it didn't seem to important at the time, that afternoon changed my whole life.

After he got our test results, the recruiter called me to say that I'd scored well. He said I could enlist and be guaranteed to get into virtually any Air Force specialty I wanted. I told him I'd think about it.

Several weeks later, my pal Mason told me he had decided to join the Air Force. Plus, he wanted me to go with him. The Air Force's "Buddy Program" guaranteed we'd be in the same flight for Basic Training. I can still remember him punching my shoulder and yelling, "Come on, this will be the biggest adventure of your life!" I told him I'd think about it. And the next day, I said "yes."

I was a mediocre student, but I was pretty good at taking standardized tests. I read an awful lot when I was a kid (anything but textbooks), and that was probably the main reason I was so good at tests. A huge part of the score you need to get into the service is based solely on your word knowledge and reading comprehension. (We will break this down further in the next section of this book.)

My biggest weakness was always math, where I barely managed to scrape by. If I had spent a week brushing up on pre-algebra before taking the ASVAB, I could have raised my ASVAB score a lot.

So my advice is: if you're thinking of joining the military—if it's a possibility at all—call a recruiter and take the ASVAB sooner rather than later. You'll feel a lot less pressure than if you wait until the last possible minute. If you don't score well, you can study some more, and retake the ASVAB.

That brings me to the whole point of this book: It's up to you. You can raise your ASVAB score. You aren't born with a certain ability to take tests, it's something you develop, like throwing a ball. You can improve your ASVAB score a lot, just by spending one week brushing up on what you've already seen in high school.

On the cover of this book, I advertised that you can "ace" the ASVAB with one week of study. That might sound too good to be true, but it is. You're not going to answer every question correctly, but you're going to (1) score well enough to enlist, and (2) score well enough to qualify for a military job that you want.

I developed ASVAB Cram to let people maximize their chance at a great military career without wasting a lot of time and money. Give it a week, then give the ASVAB your bests shot.

Maybe you've got more than a week to prepare for the ASVAB. In that case, if you're having trouble with a particular topic, look at my "Further Reading" note at the bottom of every page. Here I mention free, valuable resources—online textbooks and courses. The free textbooks have indexes at the end, so you can quickly find specific information on exactly the topic you need more study with.

You'll get there. If you had the motivation to buy this book, you're already that much closer. If I did it, so can you. As the Marine Corps General Jim Mattis famously said, "I don't lose any sleep at night over the potential for failure. I cannot even spell the word."

So that's my two cents' worth. I'll climb down off my soapbox now. But if you have something to say—any questions, concerns, feedback, or whatnot, please drop me a line at ASVABcram@weberbooks.com . I'd love to hear from you.

—Steve Weber

► INSIDE THE ASVAB

The ASVAB (Armed Services Vocational Aptitude Battery) is the qualification test for enlistment in the U.S. Armed Forces and helps determine what kind of job you'll qualify for. Usually it's taken by high school students in grades 10 through 12, although anyone eligible to join the military may take it.

The date and location of ASVAB tests in your area are available through your local recruiting office or your high school academic advisor. To locate a recruiter, visit www.todaysmilitary.com/request-information.

The ASVAB is a multiple-choice test that results in a percentile rank – if you score 75, that means you scored better than 75 of the test takers. The test is taken on a computer at military processing stations across the country, and much less frequently in a paper-and-pencil format in some military entrance sites, high schools, and colleges.

The computerized test has nine sections, called "subtests," which have a certain number of questions and a time limit, as follows:

COMPUTERIZED FORMAT

General Science (GS) – 16 questions in 8 minutes

Arithmetic Reasoning (AR) – 16 questions in 39 minutes

Word Knowledge (WK) – 16 questions in 8 minutes

Paragraph Comprehension (PC) – 11 questions in 22 minutes

Mathematics Knowledge (MK) – 16 questions in 8 minutes

Electronics Information (EI) – 16 questions in 8 minutes

Automotive Information (AI) – 7 questions in 11 minutes

Shop Information (SI) – 11 questions in 6 minutes

Mechanical Comprehension (MC) – 16 questions in 20 minutes

Assembling Objects (AO) – 16 questions in 16 minutes

PAPER FORMAT

General Science (GS) – 25 questions in 11 minutes

Arithmetic Reasoning (AR) – 30 questions in 36 minutes

Word Knowledge (WK) – 35 questions in 11 minutes

Paragraph Comprehension (PC) – 15 questions in 13 minutes

Mathematics Knowledge (MK) – 25 questions in 24 minutes

Electronics Information (EI) – 20 questions in 9 minutes

Automotive and Shop Information (AS) – 25 questions in 11 minutes

Mechanical Comprehension (MC) – 25 questions in 19 minutes

Assembling Objects (AO) – 25 questions in 15 minutes

Navy personnel take an additional test called "Coding Speed."

The big, first hurdle: your AFQT

Two scores that result from your ASVAB test. One is the general score—the AFTQ (short for Armed Forces Qualification Test)—which determines whether you can enlist. The AFTQ is a sum of your scores on the subtests Word Knowledge, Paragraph Comprehension, Arithmetic Reasoning, and Mathematics Knowledge.

So the two language-related subtests, added to the two math-related subtests, determine whether you can enter the service or not. The rest of your scores on subtests like science, mechanical knowledge and others, determine what kind of military job you'll qualify for. All of these subtests add up to your total ASVAB percentage.

This means you don't have to obsess over every subtest on the ASVAB. For example, let's say that you're aiming for a job in vehicle maintenance. Then you'd want to focus your test-prep on the Automotive Information subtest, and you could safely keep the General Science subtest on the back burner.

Your AFQT puts you into one of eight categories. If your score is between 93 percent and 99 percent, you're placed in the top rank, Category I. (The highest possible score is 99 percent.)

Category I: 93–99

Category II: 65–92

Category III A: 50–64

Category III B: 31–49

Category IV A: 21–30

Category IV B: 16–20

Category IV C: 10–15

Category V: 0–9

What's my ASVAB score?

Your ASVAB is a percentage score based on how many questions you answer correctly. But it's impossible to predict what your ASVAB score will be based on practice tests. One reason is that the computerized ASVAB test will present you with progressively more difficult questions as you guy. When you answer a question correctly, the next questions will be harder, and you'll get a higher score if you successfully answer these harder questions.

Minimum scores for enlistment eligibility

Your eligibility for enlistment depends on your ASVAB percentage score, the military branch you're applying for.

The minimal score for the Army is 31, Marines is 32, Air Force is 36, Navy is 31, Coast Guard is 36, Army National Guard is 50, and Air National Guard is 50. These minimum scores are sometimes adjusted up or down based on how well the service is meeting its recruiting goals. You can verify the current requirements by calling your local recruiting office.

Strategies for taking the ASVAB

The test administrator will provide instructions on taking the test and how much time you have available to complete each section. Before the test begins, you'll have the opportunity to view some sample questions and ask questions about the test.

To give yourself the best chance at a high score, get plenty of sleep the night before, and arriving at the test location a little ahead of time. You'll need to show identification for admission to the testing room. You can't use a calculator while taking the ASVAB.

While taking the computerized ASVAB, don't select your answers until you're relatively sure it's the one you want – once you've answered, you're not able to return to that question. If you're running short on time for a subtest, don't rush and answer questions haphazardly – you'll be penalized if you answer incorrectly several times in a row.

If you're taking the paper ASVAB, pass by questions you're unsure of, then if you have time, return to the questions you've skipped. Try answering every question, and if you're short on time, provide random answers if necessary, you won't be penalized for guessing.

Here are some additional tried and true strategies for test-taking:

- Read the entire question. Don't fall into the trap of assuming you know what the rest of the problem is, which can result in careless mistakes...

- Try answering the question in your mind before proceeding to the multiple-choice options. More often than not, the first answer that occurs to you is the correct one. Rushing through the multiple-choice options can sometime convince you that the first answer that came to your mind is incorrect.

- If you're unsure of the answer, consider all of the possible options and eliminate the ones that are obviously incorrect. This process of elimination makes it more likely you'll select the right answer.

Fighting test anxiety

If you're feeling apprehensive about taking the ASVAB, you're not alone – experts call it "test anxiety," and about 35 percent of people are affected. It causes anxiety, tension, and inability to concentrate. In serious cases, it can result in shortness of breath, stomach distress, and blanking out. As a result, text anxiety can result in lower test scores than the applicant is capable of, especially when a test has such high stakes. After all, the ASVAB isn't like a midterm exam in high school, it's a crucial test that can affect your military career – or even prevent you from qualifying for the service completely.

The good news is that you can take several steps to reduce your chances of test anxiety. First, in the weeks before you're scheduled to take the ASVAB, get proper sleep, nutrition, exercise, and periods of relaxation or meditation.

Another possible stress reliever: you can re-take the ASVAB if you don't perform up to expectations. After your first test, you can take it again after one calendar month has passed. After that, you can take the ASVAB again after waiting six calendar months. Once you've performed satisfactorily, your score is effective for two years.

And, of course, you can minimize your ASVAB test anxiety by taking the practice tests associated with this book. Knowing what to expect when you're actually taking the ASVAB can minimize the chance your chances of being nervous once you start taking the test. Also, the practice tests will help refresh your memory of high-school studies, from which much of the ASVAB draws on. And if you have any remaining textbooks or notes from your school days, a quick review of them can help refresh your overall memory.

► WORD KNOWLEDGE

The Word Knowledge subtest contains 35 questions and has a time limit of 11 minutes. It's vocabulary, vocabulary, vocabulary. The reason? Language skill is perhaps the most critical skill you need to succeed in any job.

You might think there's nothing you can do to boost your vocabulary within a short period of time, but you'd be wrong. The simple act of reading—and taking the practice tests associated with this book—will help.

If you've come up against an unfamiliar word, one of the best ways to decipher it is to take it apart. Words usually contain a root word and a prefix and perhaps a suffix that you already know. Putting these pieces together will often reveal a word's meaning. A prefix (a word or partial word preceding the root word) or suffix (a word or partial word at the end of the root word) can reveal or suggest the root word, sometimes called the "stem."

To give a very simple example, consider the word "unhappy." The prefix of the word is "un," and the root word is "happy." In this case the prefix reverses the meaning of the root word – and, of course, the meaning of the complete word is "not happy."

Here is a list of the most common prefixes and their impact on root words. The list is by no means exhaustive, but a review of what's here will get the gears in your head turning.

Prefixes: their meaning and impact

Prefix	Meaning	Example
a-	"not"	aback, asymmetric, atheist
acro-	"high"	acrobatics, acrophobia, allomorphism
allo-	"other"	allocation, allogenic, allobars
alter-	"to change"	alteration, alternate, alterabiliteis
an-	"additional"	analphabet, anaerobic
ante-	"prior"	antebellum, antecedent, antechapel
anti-	"opposite"	antisocial, antifreeze, anticlimax
auto-	"by oneself or itself"	autocracy, automatic, autobiography
bi-	"two"	bisexual, bicentennial, bicameral
co-	"together"	coalition, coadapted, cohabit
contra-	"below" ; "against"	contradict, contravene, contrarian
counter-	"against"	countermeasure, counterpunch, counterpoint
de-	"negative, remove"	de-ice, decamp, deduct

Further reading: Merriam-Webster Word Games and Quizzes —www.merriam-webster.com/word-games

di-	"two"	dioxide, dichotomy, dicarbonate
ir-	"within" ; "toward" ; "marginal or not"	irregular, irresponsible, irrational
macro-	"large-scale" ; "exceptionally prominent"	macroeconomics, macrofossil, macrocosmic
mal-	"unpleasant", "not"	malcontent, maladapted, malignancy
meso-	"middle"	mesodorsal, mesoderm, mesoamerica
meta-	"self-referential"	metafiction, metacentric, metamorphic
micro-	"small-scale"	microscope, micrometer, microanalysis
mono-	"one"	monogamy, monolith, monologue
octo-	"eight"	octostyle, octosyllabic, octogenarian
over-	"excess", "too much";	overcoat, overflow, overreact
pan-	"all"	panoply, panorama, pangene
para-	"beside"; "beyond", "altered"	paragraph, paranormal, parallel
penta-	"five"	pentagon, pentameters, pentapeptide
per-	"through"; "throughout"	permeable, pervasive, perambulatory
peri-	"around"	periscope, pericranial, periplasms
poly-	"many"	polysorbate, polycentric, polytechnic

Further reading: Merriam-Webster Word Games and Quizes —www.merQuizzesebster.com/word-games

post-	"after"	postscript, postmordem, posthumous
pro-	"on behalf of" ; "before"	profess, prolong, protract
proto-	"first"; "primitive"; "precursor"	prototype, protohuman, protoplasm
pseudo-	"false", "specious"	pseudoscience, pseudoclassics, pseudomorphisms
quadri-	"four"	quadrophonic, quadriplegic, quadriceps
quasi-	"somewhat", "resembling"	quasigovernment, quasiclassical, quasinumerical
supra-	"above"	supraorbital, suprahuman, supralinguistic
tetra-	"four"	tetrachord, tetrameter, tetrameric
trans-	"across"; "connecting"	transatlantic, transsexual, transact
xeno-	"foreign"	xenophobe, xenophile, xenoliths

Suffixes, their meaning and impact

Suffix	Meaning	Example
-al	"of the kind of, condition"	deferral, arrival, testimonial
-able	"can be"	preventable, adjustable, tolerable

Further reading: Merriam-Webster Word Games and Quizzes —www.merriam-webster.com/word-games

-acity	"quality of"	opacity, tenacity
-ade	"process, product"	lemonade, promenade
-age	"process or action"	marriage, bondage, bandage
-al	"relating to"	cranial, denial
-an, ian	"belonging to, relating to"	civilian, politician, veteran
-ance	"quality of, state of"	forbearance, alliance
-ant	"person who"	defiant, informant, participant
-ar	"of, being"	molecular, granular, tubular
-arian	"person who"	vegetarian, authoritarian
-ary	"relating to"	legendary, deflationary
-ate	"state of"	captivate, impersonate, legislate
-ation	"process or action"	flirtation, legitimization
-cracy	"power, rule"	theocracy, democracy
-crat	"person with power"	autocrat, aristocrat

Further reading: Merriam-Webster Word Games and Quizes —www.merQuizzesebster.com/word-games

-cide	"to kill"	genocide, homicide, fratricide
-ectomy	"removed surgically"	mastectomy, vasectomy
-ee	"performer, receiver"	emcee, nominee, draftee
-ence	"condition, state, action"	absence, coincidence, providence
-ency	"state of, process"	emergency, tendency, clemency
-esque	"state of, process of"	grotesque, picturesque, statuesque
-ette	"small"	kitchenette, cigarette, pipette
-gamy	"union"	polygamy, bigamy
-iasis	"malady, disease"	psoriasis, elephantiasis
-iatric	"healing"	geriatric, pediatric
-ible	"able"	flexible, horrible, feasible
-ic	"relating to"	classic, drastic, dyslexic
-ion	"process"	rationalization, discontinuation, hospitalization
-ious	"quality of"	religious, ambitious, ingenious

Further reading: Merriam-Webster Word Games and Quizzes —www.merriam-webster.com/word-games

-ism	"state of"	Internationalism, communism, institutionalism
-ist	"one who does"	receptionist, technologist, psychiatrist
-ite	"believer of, resident of"	suburbanite, indefinite, franklinite
-itis	"condition"	osteoarthritis, conjunctivitis, appendicitis
-ity	"state of, quality"	activity, futility, opportunity
-ization	"to make"	miniaturization, catheterization, crystallization
-loger	"one who does"	astrologer, cataloger, mythologer
-oid	"resembles"	trapezoid, flavonoid, celluloid
-onym	"a word representing"	acronym, synonym, homonym
-opsy	"exam"	biopsy, hydropsy, necropsy
-osis	"disease, process"	halitosis, vaginosis, fibrosis
-path	"one who does, who is"	psychopath, homeopath, telepath
-pathy	"feeling of"	sympathy, empathy, apathy
-phone	"sound"	xylophone, telephone, saxophone

Further reading: Merriam-Webster Word Games and Quizes —www.merQuizzesebster.com/word-games

-phyte	"small	Neophyte, halophyte, dermatophyte
-scope	"visual"	telescope, kinescope, periscope
-sect	"to cut"	dissect, intersect, trisect
-sophy	"knowledge, wisdom"	Philosophy, theosophy, mysteriosophy
-trophy	"growth, feeding"	Heterotrophy, dystrophy, autotrophy
-tude	"condition, quality, state"	latitude, finitude, solitude
-ular	"resembling, relating to"	cardiovascular, extracurricular, extracellular
-uous	"quality of, state"	virtuous, strenuous, ingenuous
-ware	"of the same material, type"	silverware, giftware, freeware

Root words

If you remove prefixes and suffixes from a word, you're left with the root word. Many English words are based on a root derived from a Greek or Latin word. For example, the Greek root **graph** – the English translation is **writing**. And the graph **root**, when combined with prefixes or suffixes, forms the basis of are added, is the basis of the English words **autograph**, **cartography**, **photograph**, **paragraph**, **biography**, **bibliography**, and many others. Let's take a look at more root words:

Further reading: Merriam-Webster Word Games and Quizzes —www.merriam-webster.com/word-games

Greek root words

Prefix	Meaning	Example
anti	against, apposed to	antithesis, antipathy, antisocial
ast	star	astronaut, astronomy, asterik
aqua	water	aquarium, aquifer, aqueduct
biblio	book	bibliophile, bibliophobia, bibliotherapy
bio	life	biodiversity, biomass, biotech
chrono	time	chronicle, synchrony, synchronize
geo	earth	geology, geography, geometry
gno	know	cognizant, incognito, cognoscenti
hetero	different	heterosexual, heterogeneous, heterology
logos	study	logomania, logogram, logographer
path	feel	empathy, sympathy, apathy
phil	love	philanthropy, philosophy, philharmonic
schem	plan	scheme, schematic, schema

Further reading: Merriam-Webster Word Games and Quizes —www.merQuizzesebster.com/word-games

Latin root words

ab	away	disabuse, abrogate, abdicate
acri	bitter	acrimonious, acerbic, acrid
audi	hear	audio, auditorium, audiology
aug	increase	augment, augur, auction
belli	war	bellicose, belligerent, rebellion
brev	short	abbreviation, brevity,
calor	heat	calorie, caloric
carn	flesh	carnal, incarnate, carnivore
ced	move	accede, recede, precede
centric	center	eccentric, concentric, egocentric
chrom	color	chromatic, chromosome, chrome
cide, cise	cut, kill	insecticide, homicide, excise, exorcise
civ	citizen	civilian, civic, civilization
clam	cry out	ccclaim, clamor, exclamation
cord, cardi	heart	discord, cardiac, cardiologist

Further reading: Merriam-Webster Word Games and Quizzes —www.merriam-webster.com/word-games

cred	believe	credible, incredulous, credence
cur	run	current, courier, concur
deca	ten	decade, decathlon, decalogue
dem	people	democracy, demographics, epidemic
dent	tooth	dentist, denture, dental
derm	skin	dermatology, hypodermic, epidermis
dict	speak	diction, dictate, edict
dorm	sleep	dormant, dormitory
endo	inside	Endocardial, endorse, endoskeletal
equi	equal	equilibrium, equinox
fid	faithful	fidelity, infidel, confidante
gast	stomach	gastritis, gastronomy, gastric
germ	essential part	germ, germane
grad, gress	step	Graduate, egress, progress
greg	group	congregation, gregarious, segregate

Further reading: Merriam-Webster Word Games and Quizes —www.merQuizzesebster.com/word-games

leg	law	legitimate, legal, legislate
levi	light	levitate, alleviate, levity
liber	free	deliver, liberty, liberate
liter	letters	literary, literature, illiterate
magn	big	magnify, magnate, magnitude
medi	halfway	mediocre, medieval, medium
migra	wander	migrate, immigrate, immigrant
morph	form	metamorphosis, morpheme, emorphous
oligo	small amount	oligarchy, oligotrophic
omni	pervasive	omnipresent, omnipotent, omnivorous
paleo	old	paleolithic, paleobotany, paleographical
pend	hang	appendage, suspend, pendant
poli	city, smooth	metropolis, polish, polite
pot	power	Potent, potential, impotent
rog	ask	interrogate, interrogative

Further reading: Merriam-Webster Word Games and Quizzes —www.merriam-webster.com/word-games

sci	know	conscious, science, prescient
solv	loosen	dissolve, resolve, absolve
tempo	time	temporary, contemporary, temporal
tort	twist	contort, distort, retort
tox	poison	toxic, toxin, intoxicated
trib	pay	tribute, tributary, contribute
vac	empty	vacuum, vacant, vacuous
ven	com	advent, circumvent, convene
vid	see	visit, vision, revise
voc	call	invoke, vocalize, evoke
zo	animal	zoology, protozoan, zoological

Using context to determine a word's meaning

Many of the ASVAB word knowledge questions are in the form of a sentence. Parts of the sentence can provide context – clues about an unfamiliar word's meaning.

Synonyms

For example, consider the following question.

Further reading: Merriam-Webster Word Games and Quizes —www.merQuizzesebster.com/word-games

The crime she committed was **egregious**, it is a horrible stain on her reputation.

What is the meaning of egregious?

In this sentence, we find the adjective "horrible," and that is our clue to the meaning of "egregious." The meanings of "horrible" are **shocking**, **unpleasant**, and **dreadful**, among others. These words are synonyms (meaning they have similar meanings) of "horrible." And that is our clue that the meaning of egregious is **negative**, **nasty**, and **awful**. All of these are synonyms of the word egregious and reliable clues to the question.

Antonyms

The opposite of a synonym is an **antonym**, another way we might use context to determine the meaning of a word. Consider this sentence:

Marty was **intransigent**, unlike his brother, who was always ready to compromise.

In this sentence, we see the adjective "compromise," and that Marty's brother is **unlike** intransigent. So, we can determine the meaning of **intransigent** by considering the opposite meanings of **compromise**, such as **rigid, inflexible, immovable, and uncooperative**.

Explanations

Sometimes a sentence will provide an obvious explanation of a word's meaning. Let's consider this sentence:

A **melee** broke out in the crowd, and the police were called to break up the scuffle.

In this example, we see a verb – an action was taken to resolve the situation – the police **broke up the scuffle**. And that little phrase provides a handy explanation for the meaning of **melee**. It's a **clash, a fracas, a brawl, a battle**.

Punctuation

A sentence might contain some punctuation marks – like commas, parentheses, italics or dashes –that show the meaning of a word. Let's take this sentence:

Henry is an **idealist** (a big dreamer) and makes no apologies for it.

In this case, the words between the parentheses, **a big dreamer**, are a dead giveaway to the definition of **idealist**. It can mean any of the following: escapist, daydreamer, romantic, and fantasizer.

Cause and effect

The action represented by a sentence can be a clue to a word's meaning. Let's consider:

The **conflagration** was unrelenting, every building on the block was burned to the ground.

What happened in this sentence? A whole lot of burning. And, of course, that's the definition for **conflagration – fire, blaze, inferno, wildfire**.

Sample ASVAB questions

Here are some examples of the sort of questions you'll see on ASVAB subtests. Even though you're unlikely to encounter any exact combination of questions and answers when you take the ASVAB, running through these examples lets you know what to expect in general. As a result, you can minimize the chance of being caught off guard or confused by any of the ASVAB subtests.

Remember, you have access to several full-length practice tests at ASVABcram.com.

Further reading: Merriam-Webster Word Games and Quizzes —www.merQuizzesebster.com/word-games

Word knowledge

1. **<u>Vendetta</u>** most nearly means:

a. Associate

b. Sentimental

c. Blood feud

d. Healthy body

(correct answer is c, Blood feud.)

2. The student was thorough, she took **<u>copious</u>** notes.

What does the word copious mean?

a. Abundant

b. Obscure

c. Rare

d. Meaningful

(correct answer is a, Abundant.)

3. The senile professor's lecture was **<u>opaque</u>**.

a. Redundant

b. Obvious

c. Nontransparent

d. Naïve

(correct answer is c, Nontransparent.)

4. **Pedotrophy** most nearly means:

a. Skeptical

b. Nourishment of children

c. Bawdy

d. Bicycle race

(correct answer is b, Nourishment of children.)

.

► PARAGRAPH COMPREHENSION

The Paragraph Comprehension subtest has 10 questions with a time limit of 27 minutes. This part of the ASVAB builds on the Word Knowledge we discussed in the previous section.

You can boost your Paragraph Comprehension simply by practicing reading, both for study and pleasure. Start reading newspapers. Magazines. Even reading an action novel will help boost your reading speed and understanding of all sorts of topics.

Remove distractions. There's no way you're going to read as effectively as you can while a TV, radio or any other device is blaring in the background.

Don't sell yourself short. Somewhere along the line, you might have gotten it into your head that you're a poor reader. Maybe that's right, and maybe it isn't. Anyway, if you really are below average, look at it as an opportunity. It's something you can and will get better at.

Paragraphs: the building blocks of fiction and nonfiction

Paragraphs are the building blocks of any novel, essay, research report, or any other kind of writing. Each paragraph deals with one general idea of the author's.

Paragraphs can consist of single indented sentence, but most often they are a sequence of several sentences that contain these elements:

The **topic sentence** – is the first words of a paragraph, and introduces the idea or topic of the paragraph.

Supporting sentences are the body of a paragraph that come after the topic sentence and before the concluding sentence. These sentences contain the details that illustrate the paragraph's topic.

The **concluding sentence** is a paragraph's last sentence. It restates the paragraph's topic and resolves the issues brought up in the paragraph.

Sometimes the meaning of a paragraph is literally spelled out in its sentences. Other times, you have to "read between the lines" to absorb the underlying meaning of the passage.

As an example, let's consider this paragraph from Mark Twain's *Adventures of Huckleberry Finn:*

I set down again, a-shaking all over, and got out my pipe for a smoke; for the house was all as still as death now, and so the widow wouldn't know. Well, after a long time I heard the clock away off in the town go boom—boom—boom—twelve licks; and all still again—stiller than ever. Pretty soon I heard a twig snap down in the dark amongst the trees—something was a stirring. I set still and listened. Directly I could just barely hear a "me-yow! me-yow!" down there. That was good! Says I, "me-yow! me-yow!" as soft as I could, and then I put out the light and scrambled out of the window on to the shed. Then I slipped down to the ground and crawled in among the trees, and, sure enough, there was Tom Sawyer waiting for me.

Quite a lot is packed into the first line, the topic sentence: Huck explains what he's doing and what he's experiencing—the surroundings are quiet and spooky, his mood is nervous, and he wants to secretly smoke his pipe without the widow knowing.

The following six sentences are the supporting sentences. We see the action continuing—the sounds of a clock far away, then the noise from a nearby tree, then Huck's escape through the window.

Between the lines, we sense that Huck is breaking free—from oppression to freedom, with the concluding sentence shows the arrival of his best friend and adventure companion, Tom Sawyer.

Use a dictionary

During your reading, if you come across an unfamiliar word, look it up immediately in a dictionary. It's tempting to skim over hard words, but absorbing definitions of new words will add a worthwhile boost to your overall reading skills. Keep a dictionary within reach while you're reading so that it's not too inconvenient to interrupt your reading to learn a new definition. If you don't have a dictionary, you can get an excellent paperback edition for about $4. An excellent one is Merriam Webster's Vocabulary Builder.

Looking up a word benefits you more than you might think. It not only helps your comprehension of that single word, but it exposes you to root words, prefixes and suffixes that help you readily understand many more words.

By the way, one of the best features of Amazon's Kindle e-book tablet is its built-in dictionary. Whenever you encounter an unfamiliar word, you simply tap your finger on the text, and the device instantly displays a definition—so you don't spend time thumbing through a paper dictionary. The entry-level Kindle costs about $90 nowadays and comes with a built-in dictionary and a backlight enabling you to read anywhere, even in bed with the lights out. And believe it or not, you can borrow Kindle e-books from most public libraries these days, even current bestsellers. By the time you've borrowed a dozen books, you've probably paid for the cost of your Kindle, and then some. Meanwhile you've turbocharged your vocabulary.

Start over again

If you're struggling with a passage—or if you reach the end of a paragraph and feel a little lost—force yourself to re-read the whole section. The most important part of reading is absorbing the meaning as best you can, not hurrying to finish.

Further reading: 12th Grade Language Arts — ixl.com/ela/grade-12
Reading Comprehension Practice Tests— testpreview.com/modules/reading1.htm

Going slow and understanding is a big improvement over skimming and not retaining anything. Some people try to stigmatize slow readers as dim-witted, but that's simply not true. Slow readers are often the people who understand and retain the most information.

If you're having a mental block while reading, sometimes reading out loud will help—or saying it out loud in your head.

Talking about the thing you're reading helps you focus and figure things out. So talk about it to a friend—even if it's your dog or an imaginary friend in your head.

Lots of so-called experts on reading comprehension argue that you're not supposed to vocalize the words in your head, that the "correct way" to read is by skimming through a whole sentence at a time, not one word at a time. But it doesn't really matter exactly how you go about reading, as long as you get it done. Speed-reading is way, way overrated.

Sample questions for Paragraph Comprehension

1. Negotiation is a dialogue between two or more parties aimed to arrive at a satisfactory outcome over one or more conflicting issues. To advance the negotiations, the parties must compromise on issues of mutual interest while optimizing their individual interests. All of the parties, or some of the parties, can arrive at a beneficial outcome. The degree of trust in each party to carry through on the negotiated solutions greatly determines if the negotiations are successful.

According to the passage, what is the most important factor in advancing negotiations?

a. Cunning

b. Aggressiveness

c. Compromise

d. Language

(correct answer is c, Compromise)

2. Cancer involves abnormal cell growth with the potential to invade or spread to other parts of the body. Symptoms include a lump, abnormal bleeding, prolonged cough, unexplained weight loss, and a change in bowel movements. Tobacco use is the cause of about 22% of cancer deaths. Another 10% are due to obesity, poor diet, lack of physical activity or excessive drinking of alcohol.

According to the passage, what personal habit could most often cause cancer?

a. Poor hygiene.

b. High fat consumption

c. Lack of exercise

d. Smoking

(correct answer is d, Smoking.)

3. It is a truth universally acknowledged, that a single man in possession of a good fortune must be in want of a wife. However little known the feelings or views of such a man may be on his first entering a neighborhood, this truth is so well fixed in the minds of the surrounding families, that he is considered as the rightful property of someone or other of their daughters.

What is the meaning of the paragraph above?

Further reading: 12th Grade Language Arts — ixl.com/ela/grade-12
Reading Comprehension Practice Tests— testprepreview.com/modules/reading1.htm

a. The men with the most economic power have shallow personalities.

b. Marriage often has little to do with love.

c. Women always know whether a man is trustworthy

d. Where you live decides how well you live.

(The correct answer is b, marriage often has little to do with live.)

4. Electric vehicles, known as EVs, were among the earliest automobiles before the invention of lightweight, powerful internal combustion engines. Several factors caused a decline in electric cars. Improved roads required a greater range than possible with EVs, and increased availability of affordable gasoline made internal combustion cars cheaper to operate over long distances. The noise emitted by ICE cars became more bearable thanks to the use of the muffler.

The author implies that gas-powered cars became more popular than EVs because:

a. Gasoline powered cars became more economical over long distances.

b. EVs had a higher purchase cost.

c. The government subsidized the production of gasoline.

d. EV batteries required frequent replacement.

► GENERAL SCIENCE

On the General Science subtest, you'll face 16 questions and a time limit of eight minutes.

This section is not included in your general AFQT score, but scoring well in science will open some special training and career opportunities in the service. Science is one field where the career potential in the military outweighs its civilian counterparts because of the military's high reliance on cutting-edge technology.

Unlike some other areas of the ASVAB, science is based strictly on evidence-based facts, not opinion. Having an understanding of scientific principles helps you absorb the scientific process, statistics, and analysis that you can use to make informed decisions in many fields.

Chemistry

Chemistry is sometimes referred to as "the central science" due to its interconnectedness with a vast array of other **STEM** disciplines (STEM stands for areas of study in the **science**, **technology**, **engineering**, and **math** fields). Chemistry and the language of chemists play vital roles in biology, medicine, materials science, forensics, environmental science, and many other fields.

The scientific method

The scientific method, illustrated below, follows these key components. It requires open inquiry and the reworking of questions and ideas in response to findings:

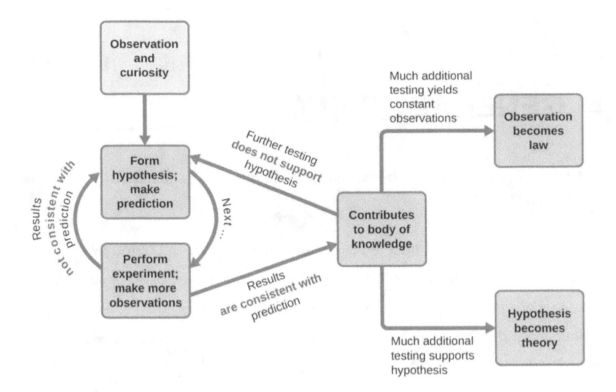

Chemists study and describe the behavior of matter and energy in three different domains: **macroscopic**, **microscopic**, and **symbolic**. These domains provide different ways of considering and describing chemical behavior.

Macro is a Greek word that means "large." The macroscopic domain is familiar to us: It is the realm of everyday things that are large enough to be sensed directly by human sight or touch. In daily life, this includes the food you eat and the breeze you feel on your face. The macroscopic domain includes everyday and laboratory chemistry, where we observe and measure physical and chemical properties such as density, solubility, and flammability.

Micro comes from Greek and means "small." The microscopic domain of chemistry is often visited in the imagination. Some aspects of the microscopic domain are visible through standard optical microscopes, for example, many biological cells. More sophisticated instruments are capable of imaging even smaller entities such as molecules and atoms.

Matter is defined as anything that occupies space and has mass, and it is all around us. Solids and liquids are more obviously matter: We can see that they take up space, and their weight tells us that they have mass. Gases are also matter; if gases did not take up space, a balloon would not inflate (increase its volume) when filled with gas.

Solids, liquids, and gases are the three states of matter commonly found on earth. A solid is rigid and possesses a definite shape. A liquid flows and takes the shape of its container, except that it forms a flat or slightly curved upper surface when acted upon by gravity. (In zero gravity, liquids assume a spherical shape.) Both liquid and solid samples have volumes that are very nearly independent of pressure. A gas takes both the shape and volume of its container.

The **law of conservation of matter** summarizes many scientific observations about matter: It states that there is no detectable change in the total quantity of matter present when matter converts from one type to another (a chemical change) or changes among solid, liquid, or gaseous states (a physical change).

Pure substances that can be broken down by chemical changes are called compounds. This breakdown may produce either elements or other compounds, or both. Mercury(II) oxide, an orange, crystalline solid, can be broken down by heat into the elements mercury and oxygen. When heated in the absence of air, the compound sucrose is broken down into the element carbon and the compound water. A summary of how to distinguish between the various major classifications of matter is illustrated below:

Further reading: Biology by Clark, Mary Ann — openstax.org/details/books/biology-2e
Anatomy and Physiology by Betts, J. Gordon — openstax.org/details/books/anatomy-and-physiology

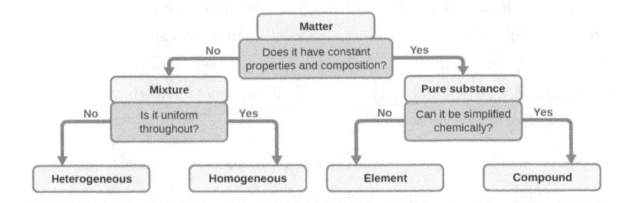

Eleven elements make up about 99% of the earth's crust and atmosphere. Oxygen constitutes nearly one-half and silicon about one-quarter of the total quantity of these elements. A majority of elements on earth are found in chemical combinations with other elements; about one-quarter of the elements are also found in the free state.

Chemical formulas

A molecular formula uses chemical symbols and subscripts to indicate the exact numbers of different atoms in a molecule or compound. An empirical formula gives the simplest, whole-number ratio of atoms in a compound. A structural formula indicates the bonding arrangement of the atoms in the molecule. Ball-and-stick and space-filling models show the geometric arrangement of atoms in a molecule. Isomers are compounds with the same molecular formula but different arrangements of atoms.

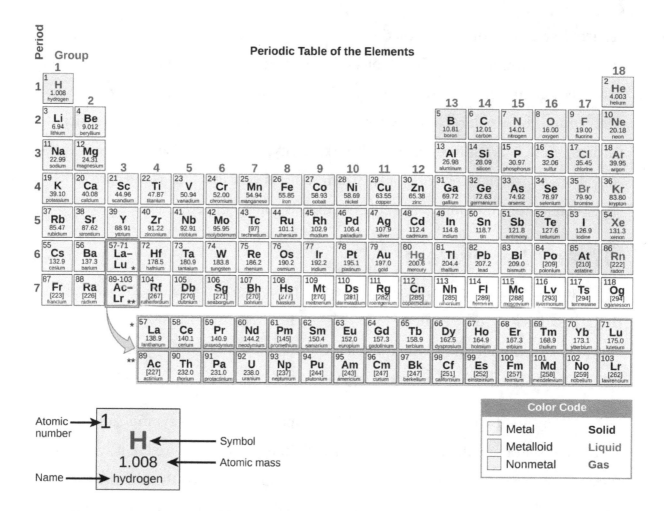

Ionic bonding

Atoms gain or lose electrons to form ions with particularly stable electron configurations. The charges of cations (positively charged ions) formed by the representative metals may be determined readily because, with few exceptions, the electronic structures of these ions have either a noble gas configuration or a completely filled electron shell. The charges of anions (negatively charged ions) formed by the nonmetals may also be readily determined because these ions form when nonmetal atoms gain enough electrons to fill their valence shells.

Covalent Bonding

Eleven elements make up about 99% of the earth's crust and atmosphere, as by the nuclei of both atoms. In pure covalent bonds, the electrons are shared equally. In polar covalent bonds, the electrons are shared unequally, as one atom exerts a stronger force of attraction on the electrons than the other. The ability of an atom to attract a pair of electrons in a chemical bond is called its **electronegativity**. The difference in electronegativity between two atoms determines how polar a bond will be. In a diatomic molecule with two identical atoms, there is no difference in electronegativity, so the bond is nonpolar or pure covalent. When the electronegativity difference is very large, as is the case between metals and nonmetals, the bonding is characterized as ionic.

The metric system

The decimal measuring system based on the meter, liter, and gram as units of length, capacity, and weight or mass. The system was first proposed by the French astronomer and mathematician Gabriel Mouton (1618–94) in 1670 and was standardized in France in the 1790s

For any given quantity whose unit has a special name and symbol, an extended set of smaller and larger units is defined that are related in a systematic system of factors of powers of ten. The unit of time should be the second; the unit of length should be either the mete or a decimal multiple of it; and the unit of mass should be the gram or a decimal multiple of it.

Measurements and the Metric System

Measurements and the Metric System

Measurement	Unit	Abbreviation	Metric Equivalent	Approximate Standard Equivalent
Length	nanometer	nm	$1\,nm = 10^{-9}\,m$	$1\,mm = 0.039\,inch$ $1\,cm = 0.394\,inch$ $1\,m = 39.37\,inches$ $1\,m = 3.28\,feet$ $1\,m = 1.093\,yards$ $1\,km = 0.621\,miles$
	micrometer	μm	$1\,\mu m = 10^{-6}\,m$	
	millimeter	mm	$1\,mm = 0.001\,m$	
	centimeter	cm	$1\,cm = 0.01\,m$	
	meter	m	$1\,m = 100\,cm$ $1\,m = 1000\,mm$	
	kilometer	km	$1\,km = 1000\,m$	
Mass	microgram	μg	$1\,\mu g = 10^{-6}\,g$	$1\,g = 0.035\,ounce$ $1\,kg = 2.205\,pounds$
	milligram	mg	$1\,mg = 10^{-3}\,g$	
	gram	g	$1\,g = 1000\,mg$	
	kilogram	kg	$1\,kg = 1000\,g$	
Volume	microliter	μl	$1\,\mu l = 10^{-6}\,l$	$1\,ml = 0.034\,fluid\ ounce$ $1\,l = 1.057\,quarts$ $1\,kl = 264.172\,gallons$
	milliliter	ml	$1\,ml = 10^{-3}\,l$	
	liter	l	$1\,l = 1000\,ml$	
	kiloliter	kl	$1\,kl = 1000\,l$	
Area	square centimeter	cm²	$1\,cm^2 = 100\,mm^2$	$1\,cm^2 = 0.155\,square\ inch$ $1\,m^2 = 10.764\,square\ feet$ $1\,m^2 = 1.196\,square\ yards$ $1\,ha = 2.471\,acres$
	square meter	m²	$1\,m^2 = 10{,}000\,cm^2$	
	hectare	ha	$1\,ha = 10{,}000\,m^2$	
Temperature	Celsius	°C	—	$1\,°C = 5/9 \times (°F - 32)$

Further reading: Biology by Clark, Mary Ann — openstax.org/details/books/biology-2e
Anatomy and Physiology by Betts, J. Gordon — openstax.org/details/books/anatomy-and-physiology

Biology

Biology is the science that studies living organisms and their interactions with one another and their environments. Science attempts to describe and understand the nature of the universe in whole or in part by rational means. Science has many fields. Those fields related to the physical world and its phenomena are natural sciences.

Science can be basic or applied. The main goal of basic science is to expand knowledge without any expectation of short-term practical application of that knowledge. The primary goal of applied research, however, is to solve practical problems.

Science uses two types of logical reasoning. Inductive reasoning uses particular results to produce general scientific principles. Deductive reasoning is a form of logical thinking that predicts results by applying general principles. The common thread throughout scientific research is using the scientific method, a step-based process that consists of making observations, defining a problem, posing hypotheses, testing these hypotheses, and drawing one or more conclusions.

Building blocks: Atoms, Isotopes, Ions, and Molecules

Matter is comprised of elements. All of the 98 elements that occur naturally have unique qualities that allow them to combine in various ways to create molecules, which in turn combine to form cells, tissues, organ systems, and organisms. Atoms, which consist of protons, neutrons, and electrons, are the smallest units of an element that retain all of the properties of that element. Electrons can transfer, share, or cause charge disparities between atoms to create bonds, including ionic, covalent, and hydrogen bonds, as well as van der Waals interactions.

Water

Water has many properties that are critical to maintaining life. It is a polar molecule, allowing for forming hydrogen bonds. Hydrogen bonds allow ions and other polar molecules to dissolve in water. Therefore, water is an excellent solvent. The hydrogen bonds between water molecules cause the water to have a high heat capacity, meaning it takes considerable added heat to raise its temperature. As the temperature rises, the hydrogen bonds between water continually break and form anew. This allows for the overall temperature to remain stable, although energy is added to the system. Water also exhibits a high heat of vaporization, which is key to how organisms cool themselves by evaporating sweat.

Water's cohesive forces allow for the property of surface tension; whereas, we see its adhesive properties as water rises inside capillary tubes. The pH value is a measure of hydrogen ion concentration in a solution and is one of many chemical characteristics that is highly regulated in living organisms through homeostasis. Acids and bases can change pH values, but buffers tend to moderate the changes they cause. These properties of water are intimately connected to the biochemical and physical processes performed by living organisms, and life would be very different if these properties were altered, if it could exist at all.

Carbon

The unique properties of carbon make it a central part of biological molecules. Carbon binds to oxygen, hydrogen, and nitrogen covalently to form the many molecules important for cellular function. Carbon has four electrons in its outermost shell and can form four bonds. Carbon and hydrogen can form hydrocarbon chains or rings. Functional groups are groups of atoms that confer specific properties to hydrocarbon (or substituted hydrocarbon) chains or rings that define their overall chemical characteristics and function.

Further reading: Biology by Clark, Mary Ann — openstax.org/details/books/biology-2e
Anatomy and Physiology by Betts, J. Gordon — openstax.org/details/books/anatomy-and-physiology
Creative Commons Attribution License v4.0

Anatomy and Physiology

Human anatomy is the scientific study of the body's structures. In the past, anatomy has primarily been studied via observing injuries, and later by the dissection of anatomical structures of cadavers, but in the past century, computer-assisted imaging techniques have allowed clinicians to look inside the living body. Human physiology is the scientific study of the chemistry and physics of the structures of the body. Physiology explains how the structures of the body work together to maintain life. It is difficult to study structure (anatomy) without knowledge of function (physiology). The two disciplines are typically studied together because form and function are closely related in all living things.

Structural Organization of the Human Body

Life processes of the human body are maintained at several levels of structural organization. These include the chemical, cellular, tissue, organ, organ system, and the organism level. Higher levels of organization are built from lower levels. Therefore, molecules combine to form cells, cells combine to form tissues, tissues combine to form organs, organs combine to form organ systems, and organ systems combine to form organisms.

The main elements that comprise the human body are shown below, from most abundant to least abundant:

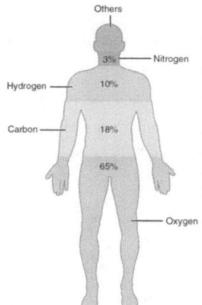

Element	Symbol	Percentage in Body
Oxygen	O	65.0
Carbon	C	18.5
Hydrogen	H	9.5
Nitrogen	N	3.2
Calcium	Ca	1.5
Phosphorus	P	1.0
Potassium	K	0.4
Sulfur	S	0.3
Sodium	Na	0.2
Chlorine	Cl	0.2
Magnesium	Mg	0.1
Trace elements include boron (B), chromium (Cr), cobalt (Co), copper (Cu), fluorine (F), iodine (I), iron (Fe), manganese (Mn), molybdenum (Mo), selenium (Se), silicon (Si), tin (Sn), vanadium (V), and zinc (Zn).		less than 1.0

Functions of Human Life

Most processes that occur in the human body are not consciously controlled. They occur continuously to build, maintain, and sustain life. These processes include: organization, in terms of the maintenance of essential body boundaries; metabolism, including energy transfer via anabolic and catabolic reactions; responsiveness; differentiation, reproduction, and renewal.

Requirements for Human Life

Humans cannot survive for more than a few minutes without oxygen, for more than several days without water, and for more than several weeks without carbohydrates, lipids, proteins, vitamins, and minerals. Although the body can respond to high temperatures by sweating and to low temperatures by shivering and increased fuel consumption, long-term exposure to extreme heat and cold is not compatible with survival. The body requires a precise atmospheric pressure to maintain its gases in solution and to facilitate respiration—the intake of oxygen and the release of carbon dioxide. Humans also require blood pressure high enough to ensure that blood reaches all body tissues but low enough to avoid damage to blood vessels.

Further reading: Biology by Clark, Mary Ann — openstax.org/details/books/biology-2e
Anatomy and Physiology by Betts, J. Gordon — openstax.org/details/books/anatomy-and-physiology

Studying Cells

A cell is the smallest unit of life. Most cells are so tiny that we cannot see them with the naked eye. Therefore, scientists use microscopes to study cells. Electron microscopes provide higher magnification, higher resolution, and more detail than light microscopes. The unified cell theory states that one or more cells comprise all organisms, the cell is the basic unit of life, and new cells arise from existing cells.

The Cell Membrane

The **cell membrane** provides a barrier around the cell, separating its internal components from the extracellular environment. It is composed of a phospholipid bilayer, with hydrophobic internal lipid "tails" and hydrophilic external phosphate "heads." Various membrane proteins are scattered throughout the bilayer, both inserted within it and attached to it peripherally. The cell membrane is selectively permeable, allowing only a limited number of materials to diffuse through its lipid bilayer. All materials that cross the membrane do so using passive (non energy-requiring) or active (energy-requiring) transport processes. During passive transport, materials move by simple diffusion or by facilitated diffusion through the membrane, down their concentration gradient. Water passes through the membrane in a diffusion process called osmosis. During active transport, energy is expended to assist material movement across the membrane in a direction against their concentration gradient. Active transport may take place with the help of protein pumps or through the use of vesicles.

The illustration below shows the generalized structure of a prokaryotic cell. All prokaryotes have chromosomal DNA localized in a nucleoid, ribosomes, a cell membrane, and a cell wall.

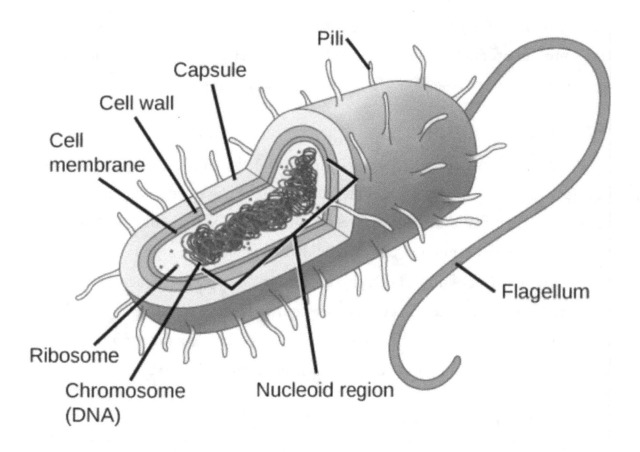

Cytoplasm and Cellular Organelles

The internal environmental of a living cell is made up of a fluid, jelly-like substance called cytosol, which consists mainly of water, but also contains various dissolved nutrients and other molecules. The cell contains an array of cellular organelles, each one performing a unique function and helping to maintain the health and activity of the cell. The cytosol and organelles together compose the cell's cytoplasm. Most organelles are surrounded by a lipid membrane similar to the cell membrane of the cell. The endoplasmic reticulum (ER), Golgi apparatus, and lysosomes share a functional connectivity and are collectively referred to as the endomembrane system.

There are two types of ER: smooth and rough. While the smooth ER performs many functions, including lipid synthesis and ion storage, the rough ER is mainly responsible for protein synthesis using its associated ribosomes. The rough ER sends newly made proteins to the Golgi apparatus where they are modified and

Further reading: Biology by Clark, Mary Ann — openstax.org/details/books/biology-2e
Anatomy and Physiology by Betts, J. Gordon — openstax.org/details/books/anatomy-and-physiology
Creative Commons Attribution License v4.0

packaged for delivery to various locations within or outside of the cell. Some of these protein products are enzymes destined to break down unwanted material and are packaged as lysosomes for use inside the cell.

Human Genetics

Genes are sequences of DNA that code for a particular trait. Different versions of a gene are called alleles—sometimes alleles can be classified as dominant or recessive. A dominant allele always results in the dominant phenotype. In order to exhibit a recessive phenotype, an individual must be homozygous for the recessive allele. Genes affect both physical and psychological characteristics. Ultimately, how and when a gene is expressed, and what the outcome will be—in terms of both physical and psychological characteristics—is a function of the interaction between our genes and our environments.

Cells of the Nervous System

Glia and neurons are the two cell types that make up the nervous system. While glia generally play supporting roles, the communication between neurons is fundamental to all of the functions associated with the nervous system. Neuronal communication is made possible by the neuron's specialized structures. The soma contains the cell nucleus, and the dendrites extend from the soma in tree-like branches. The axon is another major extension of the cell body; axons are often covered by a myelin sheath, which increases the speed of transmission of neural impulses. At the end of the axon are terminal buttons that contain synaptic vesicles filled with neurotransmitters.

Neuronal communication is an electrochemical event. The dendrites contain receptors for neurotransmitters released by nearby neurons. If the signals received from other neurons are sufficiently strong, an action potential will travel down the length of the axon to the terminal buttons, resulting in the release of neurotransmitters into the synapse. Action potentials operate on the all-or-none principle and involve the movement of Na^+ and K^+ across the neuronal membrane.

Different neurotransmitters are associated with different functions. Often, psychological disorders involve imbalances in a given neurotransmitter system. Therefore, psychotropic drugs are prescribed in an attempt to bring the neurotransmitters back into balance. Drugs can act either as agonists or as antagonists for a given neurotransmitter system.

Parts of the Nervous System

The brain and spinal cord make up the central nervous system. The peripheral nervous system is comprised of the somatic and autonomic nervous systems. The somatic nervous system transmits sensory and motor signals to and from the central nervous system. The autonomic nervous system controls the function of our organs and glands, and can be divided into the sympathetic and parasympathetic divisions. Sympathetic activation prepares us for fight or flight, while parasympathetic activation is associated with normal functioning under relaxed conditions.

The Brain and Spinal Cord

The brain consists of two hemispheres, each controlling the opposite side of the body. Each hemisphere can be subdivided into different lobes: frontal, parietal, temporal, and occipital. In addition to the lobes of the cerebral cortex, the forebrain includes the thalamus (sensory relay) and limbic system (emotion and memory circuit). The midbrain contains the reticular formation, which is important for sleep and arousal, as well as the substantia nigra and ventral tegmental area. These structures are important for movement, reward, and addictive processes. The hindbrain contains the structures of the brainstem (medulla, pons, and midbrain), which control automatic functions like breathing and blood pressure. The hindbrain also contains the cerebellum, which helps coordinate movement and certain types of memories.

Individuals with brain damage have been studied extensively to provide information about the role of different areas of the brain, and recent advances in

Further reading: Biology by Clark, Mary Ann — openstax.org/details/books/biology-2e
Anatomy and Physiology by Betts, J. Gordon — openstax.org/details/books/anatomy-and-physiology
Creative Commons Attribution License v4.0

technology allow us to glean similar information by imaging brain structure and function. These techniques include CT, PET, MRI, fMRI, and EEG.

The Endocrine System

The glands of the endocrine system secrete hormones to regulate normal body functions. The hypothalamus serves as the interface between the nervous system and the endocrine system, and it controls the secretions of the pituitary. The pituitary serves as the master gland, controlling the secretions of all other glands. The thyroid secretes thyroxine, which is important for basic metabolic processes and growth; the adrenal glands secrete hormones involved in the stress response; the pancreas secretes hormones that regulate blood sugar levels; and the ovaries and testes produce sex hormones that regulate sexual motivation and behavior.

Astronomy

The direct evidence of our senses supports a geocentric perspective, with the celestial sphere pivoting on the celestial poles and rotating about a stationary Earth. We see only half of this sphere at one time, limited by the horizon; the point directly overhead is our zenith. The Sun's annual path on the celestial sphere is the ecliptic—a line that runs through the center of the zodiac, which is the 18-degree-wide strip of the sky within which we always find the Moon and planets. The celestial sphere is organized into 88 constellations, or sectors.

Ancient Greeks such as Aristotle recognized that Earth and the Moon are spheres, and understood the phases of the Moon, but because of their inability to detect stellar parallax, they rejected the idea that Earth moves. Eratosthenes measured the size of Earth with surprising precision. Hipparchus carried out many astronomical observations, making a star catalog, defining the system of stellar magnitudes, and discovering precession from the apparent shift in the position of the north celestial pole. Ptolemy of Alexandria summarized classic astronomy in his Almagest; he explained planetary motions, including retrograde motion, with remarkably good accuracy using a model centered on Earth. This geocentric model, based on combinations of uniform circular motion using epicycles, was accepted as authority for more than a thousand years.

The Birth of Modern Astronomy

Nicolaus Copernicus introduced the heliocentric cosmology to Renaissance Europe in his book De Revolutionibus. Although he retained the Aristotelian idea of uniform circular motion, Copernicus suggested that Earth is a planet and that the planets all circle about the Sun, dethroning Earth from its position at the center of the universe. Galileo was the father of both modern experimental physics and telescopic astronomy. He studied the acceleration of moving objects and, in 1610, began telescopic observations, discovering the nature of the Milky Way, the large-scale features of the Moon, the phases of Venus, and four moons of Jupiter. Although he was accused of heresy for his support of heliocentric cosmology, Galileo is credited with observations and brilliant writings that convinced most of his scientific contemporaries of the reality of the Copernican theory.

Below: Copernicus monument in Warsaw.

Further reading: Biology by Clark, Mary Ann — openstax.org/details/books/biology-2e
Anatomy and Physiology by Betts, J. Gordon — openstax.org/details/books/anatomy-and-physiology
Creative Commons Attribution License v4.0

Psychology

Psychology derives from the roots psyche (meaning soul) and –ology (meaning scientific study of). Thus, psychology is defined as the scientific study of mind and behavior. Students of psychology develop critical thinking skills, become familiar with the scientific method, and recognize the complexity of behavior.

Before recent times, questions about the mind were considered by philosophers, but more recently, psychology has evolved into a distinct scientific discipline. **William James** was the first American psychologist, and he was a proponent of functionalism, focused on how mental activities served as adaptive responses to an organism's environment.

Sigmund Freud believed that understanding the unconscious mind was absolutely critical to understand conscious behavior. This was especially true for individuals that he saw who suffered from various hysterias and neuroses. Freud relied on dream analysis, slips of the tongue, and free association as means to access the unconscious. Psychoanalytic theory remained a dominant force in clinical psychology for several decades.

Gestalt psychology was very influential in Europe. Gestalt psychology takes a holistic view of an individual and his experiences. As the Nazis came to power in Germany, Wertheimer, Koffka, and Köhler immigrated to the United States. Although they left their laboratories and their research behind, they did introduce America to Gestalt ideas. Some of the principles of Gestalt psychology are still very influential in the study of sensation and perception.

One of the most influential schools of thought within psychology's history was **behaviorism**. Behaviorism focused on making psychology an objective science by studying overt behavior and deemphasizing the importance of unobservable mental processes. John Watson is often considered the father of behaviorism, and B. F. Skinner's contributions to our understanding of principles of operant conditioning cannot be underestimated.

As behaviorism and psychoanalytic theory took hold of so many aspects of psychology, some began to become dissatisfied with psychology's picture of human nature. Thus, a humanistic movement within psychology began to take hold. Humanism focuses on the potential of all people for good. Both Maslow and Rogers were influential in shaping humanistic psychology.

During the 1950s, the landscape of psychology began to change. A science of behavior began to shift back to its roots of focus on mental processes. The emergence of neuroscience and computer science aided this transition. Ultimately, the cognitive revolution took hold, and people came to realize that cognition was crucial to a true appreciation and understanding of behavior.

Contemporary Psychology

Psychology is a diverse discipline that is made up of several major subdivisions with unique perspectives. **Biological psychology** involves the study of the biological bases of behavior. Sensation and perception refer to the area of psychology that is focused on how information from our sensory modalities is received, and how this information is transformed into our perceptual experiences of the world around us.

Cognitive psychology is concerned with the relationship that exists between thought and behavior, and developmental psychologists study the physical and cognitive changes that occur throughout one's lifespan. Personality psychology focuses on individuals' unique patterns of behavior, thought, and emotion. Industrial and organizational psychology, health psychology, sport and exercise psychology, forensic psychology, and clinical psychology are all considered applied areas of psychology. Industrial and organizational psychologists apply psychological concepts to I-O settings. Health psychologists look for ways to help people live healthier lives, and clinical psychology involves

Further reading: Biology by Clark, Mary Ann — openstax.org/details/books/biology-2e
Anatomy and Physiology by Betts, J. Gordon — openstax.org/details/books/anatomy-and-physiology
Creative Commons Attribution License v4.0

the diagnosis and treatment of psychological disorders and other problematic behavioral patterns. Sport and exercise psychologists study the interactions between thoughts, emotions, and physical performance in sports, exercise, and other activities. Forensic psychologists carry out activities related to psychology in association with the justice system.

ASVAB sample questions

Here are a few examples of questions you'll face on the ASVAB. Remember, you have access to several full-length practice tests at ASVABcram.com.

General Science

1. Gold is heavier than lead because:

a. It has a lighter color

b. It is easier to bend.

c. Its molecules are closer together.

d. It is more valuable.

(Correct answer is c, its molecules are closer together.)

2. 100 degrees C is equal to:

a. 200 degrees F.

b. 212 degrees F.

c. 400 degrees F.

150 degrees F.

(correct answer is b, 212 degrees F.)

3. The air surrounding a city is polluted most by **what metal** emanating from car exhaust?

a. Copper

b. Sodium

c. Aluminum

d. Lead

(correct answer is d, lead.)

4. Which of the following foods is most rich in **Vitamin C**?

a. Citrus fruits

b. Seafood

c. Lentil soup

d. Milk

(correct answer is a, citrus fruits.)

Further reading: Biology by Clark, Mary Ann — openstax.org/details/books/biology-2e
Anatomy and Physiology by Betts, J. Gordon — openstax.org/details/books/anatomy-and-physiology
Creative Commons Attribution License v4.0

► AUTO & SHOP INFORMATON

The ASVAB gives you separate subtests on Automotive and Shop information, then combines your score from the two tests into one score.

There are 11 automotive questions with a time limit of seven minutes, then 11 Shop information questions with a time limit of six minutes.

People who aren't a mechanical whiz can feel intimidated by the prospect of taking a test on automotive and shop topics. Fortunately it's not as hard as you might think. The automotive questions are fairly basic, and the shop questions often ask you to identify a pictured tool and perhaps describe what it's used for.

Another thing that might put your mind at ease: if you're sure you're not interested in a mechanical or technical career, then a middling score on Automotive & Shop Information subtest will not affect your prospects.

Conventional internal combustion engine construction

The cylinder, or the engine block, is the basic foundation of virtually all liquid-cooled engines. The block is a solid casting made of cast iron or aluminum that contains the crankcase, cylinders, coolant passages, and, in the case of flathead engines, the valve seats, ports, and guides.

The cylinders are bored right into the block. A good cylinder must be round, not varying in diameter by more than approximately 0.0005 in. (0.012 mm). The diameter of the cylinder also must be uniform for its entire length.

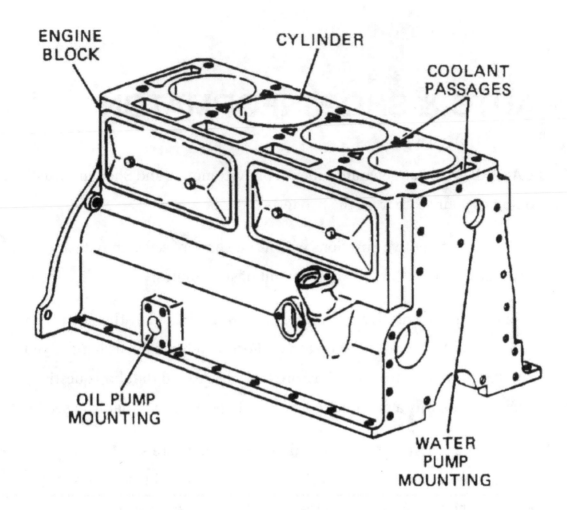

ENGINE BLOCK   CYLINDER   COOLANT PASSAGES

OIL PUMP MOUNTING   WATER PUMP MOUNTING

The connecting rods connect the pistons to the crankshaft. They must be extremely strong to transmit the thrust of the pistons to the crankshaft, and to withstand the Inertial forces of the directional changes of the pistons.

The flywheel stores energy from the power strokes, and smoothly delivers it to the drive train of the vehicle. It mounts on the end of the crankshaft, between the engine and the transmission.

Fuel system

The location of the fuel tank requires an area protected from flying debris, shielded from collision damage, and one that is not subject to bottoming. The fuel filter traps foreign material that may be present in the fuel and preventing it from entering the carburetor or sensitive fuel Injection components.

Further reading: Introduction to Automotive Technology, Editor: Levsen, Janis — www.tiny.cc/AutoStudy

The fuel pump delivers gasoline from the fuel tank to the engine. The illustration below shows a bellows-type electrical fuel pump.

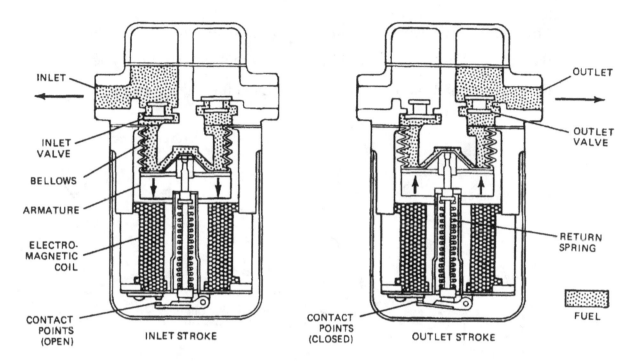

The air filter filters out any foreign matter, which would act as an abrasive between the cylinder walls and the pistons, greatly shortening engine life.

Fuel injection systems

Fuel injection systems have replaced the carburetor for providing an air-fuel mixture. They inject, under pressure, a measured amount of fuel into the intake air, usually at a point near the intake valve. Fuel injection systems provide the following advantages:

- Fuel delivery can be measured with extreme accuracy, giving the potential for improved fuel economy and performance.

- Because the fuel is injected at the intake port of each cylinder, fuel distribution will be much better and fuel condensing in the manifold will not be a problem.

Further reading: Introduction to Automotive Technology, Editor: Levsen, Janis — www.tiny.cc/AutoStudy

- There is no venturi to restrict the air intake, making it easier to keep volumetric efficiency high.

- The fuel injector, working under pressure, can atomize the fuel much finer than the carburetor, resulting in improved fuel vaporization. The illustration below shows an electronic-timed fuel injection system.

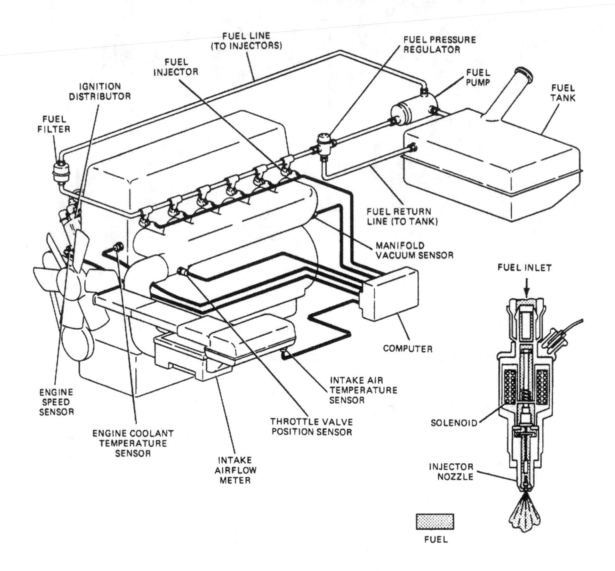

Engine oils

Engine oils generally are classified according to their performance qualities and their thickness

Further reading: Introduction to Automotive Technology, Editor: Levsen, Janis — www.tiny.cc/AutoStudy

How Oil Lubricates

- Every moving part of the engine is designed to have a specific clearance between it and its bearing. As oil is fed to the bearing it forms a film, preventing the rotating part from actually touching the bearing.

- As the part rotates, the film of oil acts as a series of rollers. Because the moving parts do not actually touch each other, friction is reduced greatly.

- It is Important that sufficient clearance be allowed between the part and the bearing. Otherwise the film might be too thin. This would allow contact between the parts, causing the bearing to wear or burn up.

- It also is important that the clearance not be too large between rotating parts and their bearings. This is true particularly with heavily loaded bearings like those found on the connecting rods. The heavy loads could then cause the oil film to be squeezed out, resulting in bearing failure.

Oil does not wear out, but it does become contaminated. When foreign matter enters through the air Intake, some of it will pass by the piston rings and enter the crankcase. This dirt, combined with foreign matter entering through the crankcase breather pipe, mixes with the oil, and when forced into the bearings, greatly accelerates wear.

Oil pumps are mounted either inside or outside of the crankcase, depending on the design of the engine. They usually are mounted so that they can be driven by a worm or spiral gear directly from the camshaft. Oil pumps generally are of the gear or the rotor type.

The oil filter removes most of the impurities that have been picked up by the oil as it is circulated through the engine. The filter is mounted outside of the engine and is designed to be replaceable readily.

Further reading: Introduction to Automotive Technology, Editor: Levsen, Janis — www.tiny.cc/AutoStudy

Cooling system

All internal combustion engines are equipped with some type of cooling system because of the high temperatures they generate during operation. High temperatures are necessary to generate the high gas pressures that act on the head of the piston. Power cannot be produced efficiently without high temperatures.

However, it is not possible to use all of the heat of combustion without harmful results. The temperature in the combustion chamber during the burning of the fuel is well above the melting point of iron. Therefore, if nothing is done to cool the engine during operation, valves will burn and warp, lubricating oil will break down, and bearings and pistons will overheat, resulting in engine seizure.

Cooling Mediums

Liquid is the most popular coolant in automotive use. A liquid cooling system provides the most positive cooling and is best for maintaining an even engine temperature.

Air cooling is most practical for small vehicles and equipment because no radiator or hoses are required. Air cooling generally will not be used wherever water cooling is practical.

A simple liquid-cooled cooling system consists of a radiator, coolant pump, piping, fan, thermostat, and a system of jackets and passages in the cylinder head and cylinder block through which the coolant circulates. Some engines are equipped with a water distribution tube inside the cooling passages that directs additional coolant to the points where the temperatures are highest. Cooling of the engine parts is accomplished by keeping the coolant circulating and in contact with the metal surfaces to be cooled.

Further reading: Introduction to Automotive Technology, Editor: Levsen, Janis — www.tiny.cc/AutoStudy

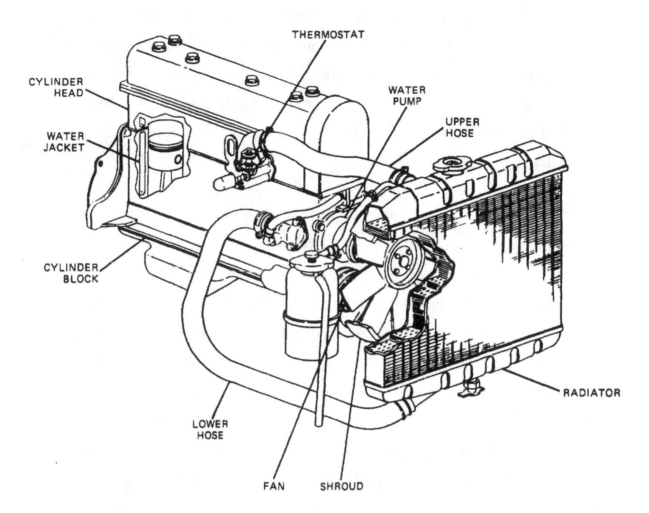

Radiators for automotive vehicles using liquid cooling systems consist of two tanks with a heat exchanging core between them. The upper tank contains an outside pipe called an inlet. The filler neck generally is placed on the top of the upper tank; attached to this filler neck is an outlet to the overflow pipe. The lower tank also contains an outside pipe that serves as the radiator's outlet.

All modern cooling systems have water pumps to circulate the coolant. The pump, usually located on the front side of the engine block, receives coolant from the lower tank and force sit through the water jacket into the upper radiator tank.

Electrical system

The storage battery provides electrical energy through chemical reactions. When a generator in the electrical system of a motor vehicle produces more electrical energy than required for ignition and for operating electrical

Further reading: Introduction to Automotive Technology, Editor: Levsen, Janis — www.tiny.cc/AutoStudy

accessories, the surplus (under certain conditions) passes through the battery to reverse the chemical reaction. This is known as charging the battery. When the generator is not producing the necessary electrical energy, the battery, through chemical reaction, can supply the energy required in the electrical system of the vehicle. The battery then is said to be discharging. The most common battery for automotive use is the lead-acid battery.

Charging system

The generator is a machine in which the principle of electromagnetic induction is used to convert mechanical energy into electrical energy. The generator restores the current used in cranking the engine to the battery. It also supplies, up to the limit of its capacity, current to carry the electrical load of the lights, ignition, radio, and horn. A generator and a motor are basically the same in construction and use the same electrical principles; however, their operation is opposite. In the generator, mechanical motion is converted into electrical energy. In the motor, electrical energy is converted into mechanical motion. Most of the military vehicles are now equipped with an AC charging system. The reason for changing to the ac system is that an alternator is capable of producing a higher voltage at idle speed, whereas a DC generator produces very little voltage at idle speed.

Many of the military vehicles are equipped with radios, firing devices, and other high-current-drawing equipment. When this equipment is in operation and the vehicle's engine is at a low rpm, a dc generator will not produce the required current and voltage to keep the batteries charged and supply the current required to operate the accessories properly.

The alternator is composed of the same basic parts as a DC generator. There is a field that is called a rotor and a generating part known as the stator. The purpose of the alternator is to produce more power and operate over a wider speed range than that of a generator. Because of this, the construction of the functional parts is different. The stator is the section in which the current is

Further reading: Introduction to Automotive Technology, Editor: Levsen, Janis — www.tiny.cc/AutoStudy

induced. It is made of a slotted laminated ring with the conductors placed in the slots. The current generated in the windings is transferred to the rest of the system through three stationary terminals

A typical alternator is shown below:

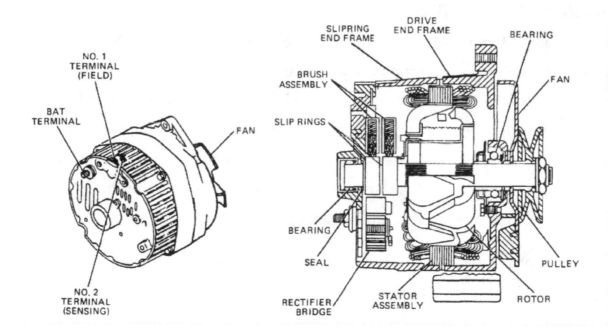

Starting system

Any internal combustion engine must be cranked manually to start it running on its own. Early automotive vehicles were started by the driver through the use of a handcrank. A system of cranking the engine with an electric motor was developed as automotive technology progressed. The modern electric starting system has reduced the task of starting an internal combustion engine to the turn of a key or the pushing of a button.

Automotive Starting Motor

In use, the motor armature has many armature coils equally spaced around the entire circumference of the armature. Each of these coils carries current and

Further reading: Introduction to Automotive Technology, Editor: Levsen, Janis — www.tiny.cc/AutoStudy

consequently exerts a force to rotate the armature as it passes the pole pieces. The switching of the armature coils to the brushes is handled by a segmented commutation. The result is a comparatively high turning power (or torque) that is sufficient to crank the engine.

Braking systems

Braking action is the use of a controlled force to accomplish the three basic tasks of reducing speed, stopping, and holding an object in a stationary position. Braking action usually is accomplished by rubbing two surfaces together that cause **friction** and heat. Friction is the resistance to relative motion between two surfaces in contact. The mechanical energy of reaction then is transformed into hear energy. Heat energy is an unwanted product of friction and must be dissipated to the surrounding environment as efficiently as possible.

Automotive vehicles use this rubbing action to develop the friction required for braking. Braking action also may be accomplished by establishing a rubbing contact with the roadway, as is done by some trolleys, which apply braking surface to the rails.

Braking Requirements

To increase a vehicle's speed requires an increase in the power output of the engine. It also is true, although not so apparent, than an increase in speed requires an increase in the braking action required to bring a vehicle to a stop

A moving vehicle, just as any other moving body, has what is known as kinetic energy. **Kinetic energy** is the energy an object possesses due to its relative motion and may be expressed as ½ (mass) x (velocity)^2. This kinetic energy, which increases with the square of the speed, must be overcome by braking action. If the speed of a vehicle is doubled, its kinetic energy is increased fourfold; four times as much energy, therefore, must be overcome by the braking action.

Further reading: Introduction to Automotive Technology, Editor: Levsen, Janis — www.tiny.cc/AutoStudy

Brakes must not only be capable of stopping a vehicle, but must stop it in as short a distance as possible. Because brakes are expected to decelerate a vehicle at a faster rate than the engine can accelerate it, they must be able to control a greater power than that developed by the engine. This is the reason that well-designed, powerful brakes have to be used to control the modern high-speed motor vehicle.

The **disk brake** system is operated hydraulically and has rotating and nonrotating components. Disk brakes can be used on all four wheels or they can be mounted on the front wheels and used in conjunction with drum brakes, which are mounted in the rear. These configurations are very popular because the disk system is a very efficient brake system, it stays cool due to its open design, and is less prone to brake fade.

The rotating member is in the form of a heavy roundshaped disk. The disk or rotor is attached to the wheel assembly and may be a solid or vented construction. The disk may be an Integral part of the hub or detachable from the hub by the use of bolts. The clamp assembly or caliper is the stationary member in the system and usually is mounted to the spindle or splash shield to provide support. The caliper is fitted with one or more pistons that are actuated hydraulically by the fluid pressure developed in the brake system. Brake pads are designed to fit into the caliper and provide the frictional surface for the rotor to engage during braking.

An example of a disk brake assembling is pictured below:

Further reading: Introduction to Automotive Technology, Editor: Levsen, Janis — www.tiny.cc/AutoStudy

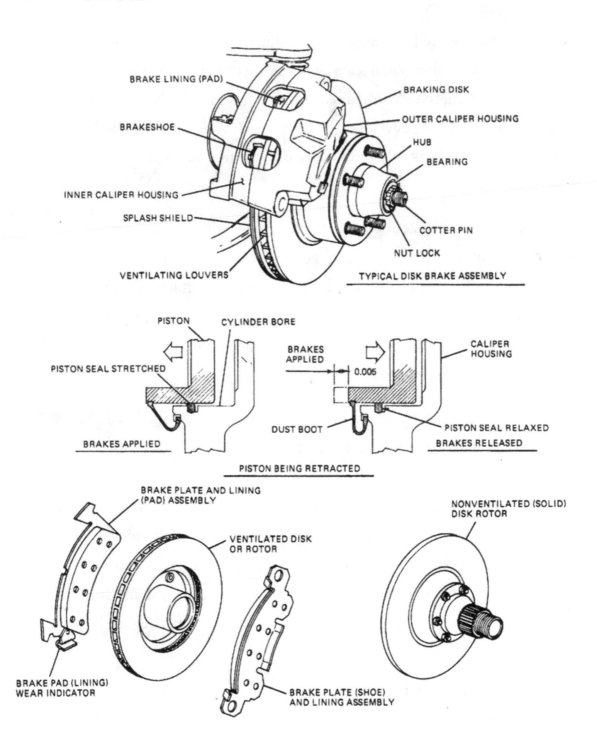

BRAKE LINING (PAD)
BRAKING DISK
OUTER CALIPER HOUSING
BRAKESHOE
HUB
BEARING
INNER CALIPER HOUSING
SPLASH SHIELD
COTTER PIN
NUT LOCK
VENTILATING LOUVERS
TYPICAL DISK BRAKE ASSEMBLY

PISTON
CYLINDER BORE
BRAKES APPLIED
CALIPER HOUSING
PISTON SEAL STRETCHED
0.005
DUST BOOT
PISTON SEAL RELAXED
BRAKES RELEASED
BRAKES APPLIED
PISTON BEING RETRACTED

BRAKE PLATE AND LINING (PAD) ASSEMBLY
NONVENTILATED (SOLID) DISK ROTOR
VENTILATED DISK OR ROTOR
BRAKE PAD (LINING) WEAR INDICATOR
BRAKE PLATE (SHOE) AND LINING ASSEMBLY

Operating Principles

The disk brake, like a drum brake assembly, is operated by pressurized. The fluid, which is routed to the calipers through steel lines and flexible high-pressure hoses, develops its pressure in the master cylinder. Once the brake pedal is depressed, fluid enters the caliper and begins to force the piston(s) outward. This

Further reading: Introduction to Automotive Technology, Editor: Levsen, Janis — www.tiny.cc/AutoStudy

outward movement forces the brake pads against the moving rotor. Once this point is reached, the braking action begins. The greater the fluid pressure exerted on the piston(s) from the master cylinder, the tighter the brake pads will be forced against the rotor. This increase in pressure also will cause an increase in braking effect. As the pedal is released, pressure diminishes and the force on the brake pads is reduced. This allows the rotor to turn more easily. Some calipers allow the brake pads to rub lightly against the rotor at all times in the released position.

Master Cylinder

The master cylinder is the primary unit in the brake system that converts the force of the driver's foot into fluid pressure to operate the wheel brake cylinders. The master cylinder housing is an aluminum or iron casting that may have an integral reservoir, in which case, it usually is made of the same material the cylinder is made of, or a detachable nylon or steel reservoir. The reservoir carries sufficient reserve fluid to allow for expansion and contraction of brake fluid and brake lining wear. The reservoir is filled at the top and is well sealed by a removable filler cap containing a vent. The master cylinder usually is mounted to the firewall, which allows for easy Inspection and service and is less prone to dirt and water.

Piston

The piston is a long, spool-like member with a rubber secondary cup seal at the outer end and a rubber primary cup that acts against the brake liquid just ahead of the Inner end. This primary cup is kept against the end of the piston by a return spring. A steel stop disk, held in the outer end of the cylinder by a retainer spring, acts as a piston stop. A rubber boot covers the piston end of the master cylinder to prevent dust and other foreign matter from entering it. This boot is vented to prevent air from being compressed within it.

Check Valve

Further reading: Introduction to Automotive Technology, Editor: Levsen, Janis — www.tiny.cc/AutoStudy

A combination inlet and outlet check valve is in the head of the master cylinder, held in place by the piston return spring. The check valve consists of a rubber valve cup in a steel valve case. This assembly rests on a rubber valve seat that fits in the end of the cylinder. In some designs, the check valve consists of a spring-operated outlet valve seated on a valve cage, rather than a rubber-cup outlet valve. The principle of operation is the same. The piston return spring normally holds the valve cage against the rubber valve seat to seal the brake fluid in the brake line.

Dual Master Cylinder

The dual master cylinder contains two brake circuits that are separated hydraulically. The individual brake systems may be designed to divide the system front to rear, diagonally, or in various other fashions. If a brake fluid leak develops in one circuit, the other circuit still provides emergency stopping capability. As the brake pedal is depressed under normal operating conditions, it forces the primary piston forward to cover the primary compensating port. At this time, the primary chamber is sealed and direct hydraulic pressure is transmitted to the secondary piston.

As the brake pedal continues to travel, the secondary piston covers the compensating port. Further application of the brake pedal develops the pressure required to apply the brake components. Should a leak develop in the primary circuit, the brake system would not be rendered useless. During the application of the brakes, the primary piston would continue to move forward, unable to build pressure due to the malfunction.

Approximately halfway through its maximum stroke, the primary piston contacts the secondary piston. Further application of the brake would force the secondary piston forward to develop pressure In the secondary system, which would allow for braking action to take place In two wheels. Should the secondary circuit fail, braking for the other two wheels would still be available. The primary piston would move forward and cover the primary compensating port as before.

Further reading: Introduction to Automotive Technology, Editor: Levsen, Janis — www.tiny.cc/AutoStudy

Below is an illustration of a master cylinder and its components:

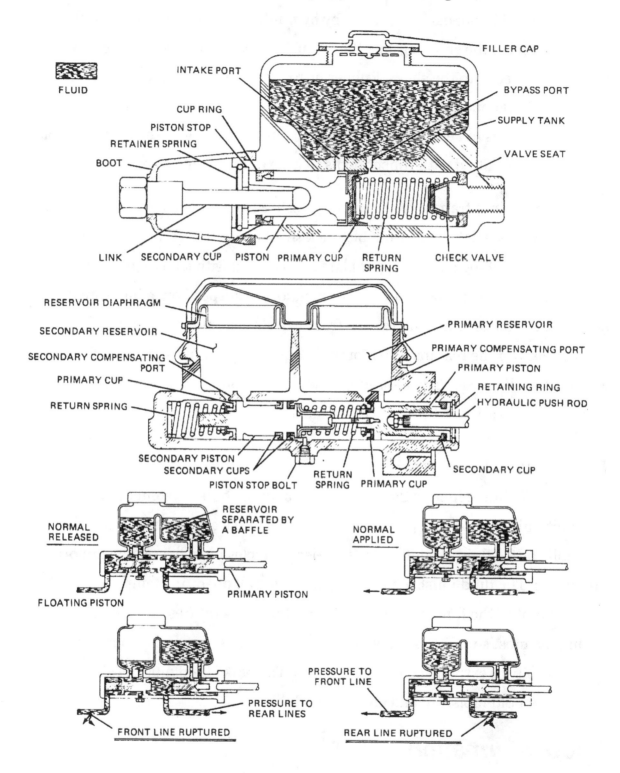

The wheel cylinder changes hydraulic pressure to the mechanical force that pushes the brake shoes against the drums. The wheel cylinder housing is a

Further reading: Introduction to Automotive Technology, Editor: Levsen, Janis — www.tiny.cc/AutoStudy

casting mounted on the brake backing plate. Inside the cylinder are two pistons that are moved in opposite directions by hydraulic pressure and which, at the same time, push the shoes against the drum. The pistons or piston stems are connected directly to the shoes. Rubber piston cups fit tightly in the cylinder bore against each piston to prevent the escape of brake liquid. There is a light spring between the cups to keep them in position against the pistons. The open ends of the cylinder are fitted with rubber boots to keep out foreign matter.

The brake lines transmit fluid under pressure from the master cylinder to the wheel cylinders. High-quality double thick steel tubing is used where no flexing is involved. The tubing also is copper plated and coated with lead to prevent rust and corrosion. Due to the relative movement of the suspension, a high-pressure hose is used to transmit fluid to each front wheel brake assembly and to the components on the rear axle(s). Mounting brackets also are used where flex hoses connect to solid hoses. The mounting brackets help hold the assemblies secure and reduce vibration, which may cause metal fatigue.

Brake Fluid

Hydraulic brake fluid is the liquid medium in the brake system used to transmit fluid motion and pressure to the wheel brake components. The hydraulic brake fluid used in today's modern vehicles must have some important properties. The fluid must remain a liquid during all operating temperatures. The boiling point of the fluid must be well above the temperatures encountered during the most severe brake application on the hottest day and also maintain an even viscosity at extreme cold temperatures. The brake fluid must be able to absorb and hold moisture and also act as a lubricant.

Shop information

As mentioned previously, the Shop Information subtest is combined with your score on the Automotive Information. This subtest gauges your knowledge of

Further reading: Introduction to Automotive Technology, Editor: Levsen, Janis — www.tiny.cc/AutoStudy

common tools. You'll have six minutes to answer 11 questions on the computerized version of the ASVAB.

Measuring tools

Steel rule

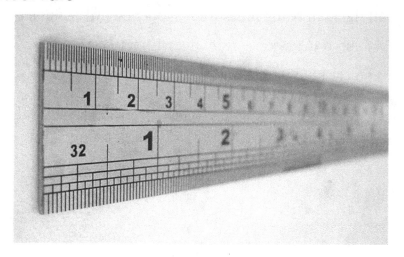

A steel rule, often called a ruler or line gauge, is used in geometry and technical drawing. They're used to measure, draw straight lines, and serve as a guide for cutting and scoring with a blade.

Steel squares, often called "carpenter's squares" or "framing squares," provide a 90-degree angle used as a guide for exact angles for frame rafters and stairs, among other things.

Micrometer

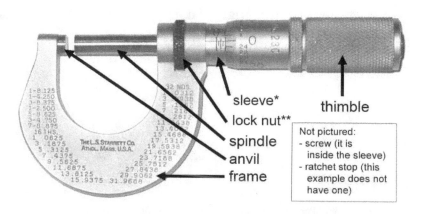

Further reading: Introduction to Automotive Technology, Editor: Levsen, Janis — www.tiny.cc/AutoStudy

Micrometers, sometimes called a "micrometer screw gauge," provide a precise measurement of components. The user turns the thimble, which is attached to a finely machined screw, until the item being measured is touched by the anvil and spindle. Micrometers are also used in astronomy, along with telescopes, to measure the distance between celestial bodies and the size of items in space.

Spirit level

Spirit levels, also called "bubble levels" or simply "levels," indicate whether a surface is horizontally level or vertical (plumb). It's used by carpenters, bricklayers, surveyors, metalworkers and others.

The measurement is made by looking at a glass tube containing a bubble. If the bubble travels to the center of the tube, the angle is correct.

Further reading: Introduction to Automotive Technology, Editor: Levsen, Janis — www.tiny.cc/AutoStudy

Calipers

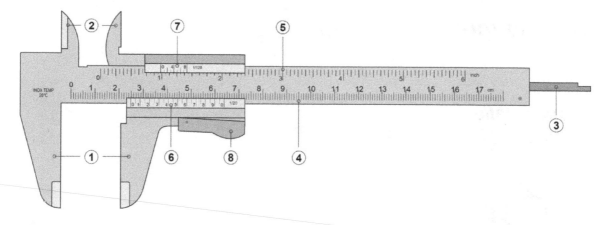

Diagram of Vernier calipers. The labeled parts are

1. **Outside large jaws**: used to measure external diameter or width of an object
2. **Inside small jaws**: used to measure internal diameter of an object
3. **Depth probe/rod**: used to measure depths of an object or a hole
4. **Main scale (Metric)**: scale marked every mm
5. **Main scale (Imperial)**: scale marked in inches and fractions
6. **Vernier scale (Metric)** gives interpolated measurements to 0.1 mm or better
7. **Vernier scale (Imperial)** gives interpolated measurements in fractions of an inch
8. **Retainer**: used to block movable part to allow the easy transferring of a measurement

Calipers measure the dimensions of an item. The tips of the caliper are adjusted to fit the item being measured and provide a distance, much like a ruler. Calipers are used in woodworking, metalworking, mechanical engineering, and other trades. "Outside calipers" are used to measure the external size of an object, and "inside calipers" measure the interior of an object.

The caliper pictured above uses a rack-and-pinion gear mechanism to move the jaws. Digital calipers are a relatively new innovation that makes the device more accurate and easy to use.

Further reading: Introduction to Automotive Technology, Editor: Levsen, Janis — www.tiny.cc/AutoStudy

Striking tools

Rubber mallet

Mallets are a hammer-like instrument, often made of rubber or wood, with a somewhat large head. They're used for woodworkers using chisels, providing a more softened strike compared to a metal hammer. The softer mallets are often used for striking machinery, reducing the chance of damaging the metal or producing sparks.

Ball peen hammer

Further reading: Introduction to Automotive Technology, Editor: Levsen, Janis — www.tiny.cc/AutoStudy

Ball-peen hammers, sometimes called a machinist's hammer, are used for metalworking. It has one flat striking surface and a rounded surface called the peen. This rounded surface is suitable for rounding off the edges of rivets and other metal fasteners. The flat face is good for striking chisels and punches.

Claw hammer

Claw hammers are used mainly for driving nails or pulling them from an object. A variation on the claw hammer, a framing hammer, is a larger hammer used for framing carpentry. Framing hammers are bigger and heavier, and can drive nails with more depth and force.

Sledge hammer

A sledgehammer has a large, heavy head attached to a long handle, enabling the user to apply heavy force for driving nails and other tasks, like demolishing drywall or masonry.

Further reading: Introduction to Automotive Technology, Editor: Levsen, Janis — www.tiny.cc/AutoStudy

Pin punch

A pin punch is a metal rod with a broad butt at one end that can be hammered. At the other end, a narrow tip concentrates the strike from a hammer down to a small area. Punches are good for marking spots or driving nails without marring the surface with a hammer head.

Rivets

Rivets are a metal fastener with a shaft on one end, and a head on the other end, called a "tail." The rivet is driven into a hole, then struck, flattening it out to a larger diameter. Rivets are used where safety and reliability are a must, such as aircraft frames and bridges. However, rivets are largely being replaced by high-strength bolts, which do not require a highly skilled installer.

Turning tools

Screwdriver

Further reading: Introduction to Automotive Technology, Editor: Levsen, Janis — www.tiny.cc/AutoStudy

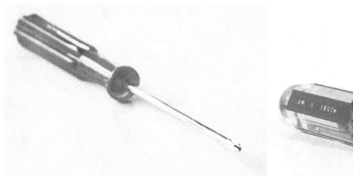

Above: a Phillips-head screwdriver, and a flathead screwdriver.

Screwdrivers are used for installing (screwing) and removing (unscrewing) screws. The tip is shaped into a driving surface to match the design of the screw's driving surface.

Wrench

Above: an adjustable wrench, an open end wrench, a combination wrench and a socket wrench.

Wrenches, or spanner tools, are used to turn rotary fasteners such as nuts and bolts. Below is an illustration of a socket wrench, sometimes called a ratchet. This allows the worker to pivot the handle back and forth to turn the socket instead of having to reposition the wrench with each turn. Socket wrenches using a pneumatic impact or hydraulic torque can do the job faster and with increased force.

Further reading: Introduction to Automotive Technology, Editor: Levsen, Janis — www.tiny.cc/AutoStudy

Pipe wrench

Pipe wrenches are used for turning threaded pipe and fittings. It's an adjustable wrench with serrated teeth that grip the softer metal of a pipe.

Bolts

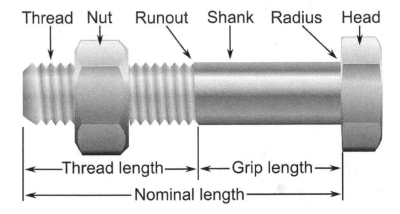

Above: a bolt and nut

Bolts are design to assemble components in conjunction with a nut. Like screws, bolt heads can have different designs, such as socket cap, hex, and slotted hex washer.

Soldering tools

Soldering is the process in which two or more items are joined using a melted filler metal into a joint. The process is used in electronics, plumbing and metalwork, among other things. A hand-held soldering iron, as shown below, can

Further reading: Introduction to Automotive Technology, Editor: Levsen, Janis — www.tiny.cc/AutoStudy

be used for small jobs, and the use of ovens can create several joints in a single process.

Gripping tools

Pliers

Above: a set of pliers and Channellock pliers. Below: Needle-nose pliers and diagonal cutters.

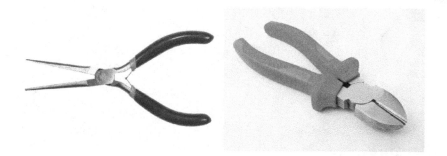

Pliers are hand tools that resemble tongs, used to hold objects together. The long handles enable the user to apply increased force at the plier's jaws. Diagonal cutters are designed for cutting instead of gripping.

Further reading: Introduction to Automotive Technology, Editor: Levsen, Janis — www.tiny.cc/AutoStudy

Vise grips

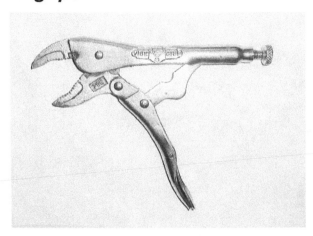

Vise grips, also called "locking pliers" can be locked into position using an over-center clamp. A bolt is used to narrow the jaws, and a spring maintains pressure on the jaws. One use of vise grips is to loosen a bolt or nut that has been worn down, or stripped.

Vise

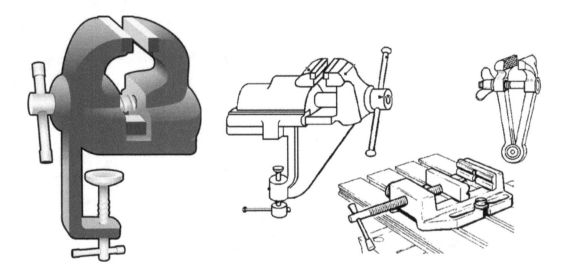

A vise, often attached to a workbench, is used to clamp an item in place so that work can be done on it. At left is a light-duty vise that might be attached to a home workbench. The illustration on the right shows (A) a bench vise, (B) a machine vise, and (C) a hand vise.

Further reading: Introduction to Automotive Technology, Editor: Levsen, Janis — www.tiny.cc/AutoStudy

Clamp

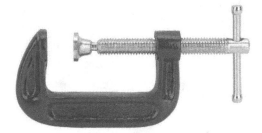

A clamp secures objects, often temporarily during construction and woodworking. Permanent clamps are used for hoses and wire ropes. The illustration above is of a "C clamp." It might be used to hold pieces of wood as they're being glued together.

Cutting tools

Hand saw

Also called "panel saws," hand saws can be used to cut wood. There are two main designs of teeth on a saw: cross cut, for cutting across the wood's grain, and rip teeth, for cutting with the grain.

Hacksaw

Hacksaws are usually handheld fine-toothed saws made for cutting metal. Similar designs for cutting wood are called a "bow saw."

Most hacksaws have a C-shaped frame holding a blade that is held under tension using a screw or another device.

Coping saw

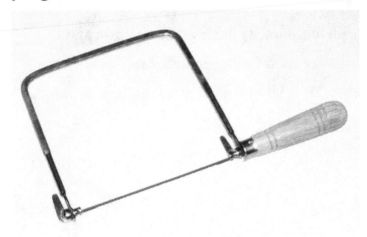

Coping saws are bow saws used to cut shapes and cutouts of wood. Coping saws are often used to cut moldings. Unlike a hacksaw, the coping saw blade's teeth are pointing toward the handle, and cuts on the pull stroke. A coping saw can be used to cut metal, though a hacksaw is usually more efficient.

Powered miter saw

Further reading: Introduction to Automotive Technology, Editor: Levsen, Janis — www.tiny.cc/AutoStudy

A miter saw, also called a "chop saw," is used for crosscuts and miters by positioning a mounted blade onto a piece of wood.

A power miter saw, also called a "drop saw," is a power tool for making accurate crosscuts in wood at a precise angle.

Miter box

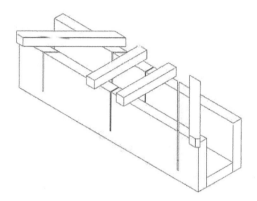

Miter boxes are used to guide a handsaw mile making price miter cuts in a piece of wood. The cut starts with the saw bladed placed in the slot and moving the saw back and forth.

Drilling tools

Handheld drill

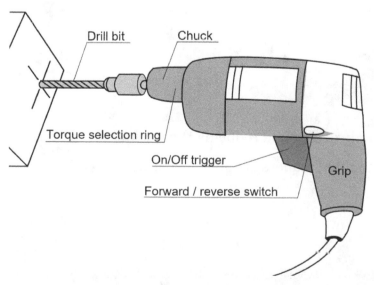

Further reading: Introduction to Automotive Technology, Editor: Levsen, Janis — www.tiny.cc/AutoStudy

A drill can be used to make round holes or to drive screws and other fasteners. Cordless, battery powered models are increasingly popular.

Drill press

Drill presses can be mounted on a pedestal or bench. Compared to a portable drill, a drill press offers more accuracy and less effort.

Finishing tools

Planers

Jack planes are used for woodworking and reducing the thickness of a board. Electric-powered and bench-mounted planers are also available.

Chisel

Chisels are used for carving or cutting wood, stone, metal or other material. The butt of the chisel can be struck with a mallet or hammer.

33

Files and rasps

Files and rasps are a hand tool tapered with a rough surface for coarsely shaping wood or other material. In woodworking, these instruments precede the use of sandpaper.

Sample ASVAB questions

Here are some examples of the sort of questions you'll see on ASVAB subtests.

Remember, you have access to several full-length practice tests at ASVABcram.com.

Automotive Information

1. Following any chassis or suspension work, what does a car need?

a. Tire rotation

Further reading: Introduction to Automotive Technology, Editor: Levsen, Janis — www.tiny.cc/AutoStudy

b. Coolant flush

c. Alignment

d. New rotors

(Correct answer is c, Alignment.)

2. What component is tested during an emissions inspection?

a. Brake Pads

b. Catalytic Converter

c. Radiator Hose

d. Shock Absorbers

(Correct answer is b, Catalytic Converter.)

3. What is the primary function of the alternator?

a. Charging the Battery

b. Regulating Transmission

c. Balancing Tires

d. Cooling the Engine

(Correct answer is a, Charging the Battery.)

Further reading: Introduction to Automotive Technology, Editor: Levsen, Janis — www.tiny.cc/AutoStudy

4. What is the usual tire pressure for a passenger car?

a. 50 to 75 psi

b. 150 to 175 psi

c. 32 to 35 psi

d. 8 to 10 psi

(correct answer is c, 32 to 35 psi.)

Shop Information

1. What handsaw is used to make a rough cut with the grain in a thick board?

a. Hacksaw

b. Crosscut Saw

c. Coping Saw

d. Ripsaw

(correct answer is d, Ripsaw.)

2. What item is best for measuring a piece of wood's full length?

a. Tape Measure

b. Triangle

c. Level

d. Screw Gauge

(Correct answer is a. Tape Measure

3. The number of teeth per inch on a saw is known as:

a. Points per inch

b. Grit

c. Surface number

d. Points per tool inch

Correct answer is a, points per inch.

4. What grit of sandpaper is best for removing rust?

a. 320

b. 725

c. 25

d. 1050

(Answer is a, 320.)

Further reading: Introduction to Automotive Technology, Editor: Levsen, Janis — www.tiny.cc/AutoStudy

► MECHANICAL COMPREHENSION

Take a quick look around, and you'll probably see half a dozen machines that you don't recognize as such. Ordinarily you think of a machine as a complex device—a gasoline engine or a computer. They are machines; but so are a hammer, a screwdriver, and a doorknob. A machine is any device that helps you to do **work**. A claw hammer, for example, is a machine. You can use it to apply a large force for pulling out a nail; a relatively small pull on the handle produces a much greater force at the claws.

We use machines to transform energy. For example, a generator transforms mechanical energy into electrical energy. We use machines to transfer energy from one place to another. For example, the connecting rods, crankshaft, drive shaft, and rear axle of an automobile transfer energy from the engine to the rear wheels. Another use of machines is to **multiply** force. We use a system of pulleys (a chain hoist, for example) to lift a heavy load. The pulley system enables us to raise the load by exerting a force that is smaller than the weight of the load. We must exert this force over a greater distance than the height through which the load is raised, so the load will move slower than the chain we pull on. The machine enables us to gain force, but only at the expense of speed.

Machines may also be used to multiply speed. The best example of this is the bicycle, by which we gain speed by exerting a greater force. Machines are also used to change the direction of a force.

There are only six **simple machines**: the lever, the block, the wheel and axle, the inclined plane, the screw, and the gear. Physicists, however, recognize only two basic principles in machines: those of the lever and the inclined plane.

The wheel and axle, block and tackle, and gears may be considered levers. The wedge and the screw use the principle of the inclined plane.

When you are familiar with the principles of these simple machines, you can readily understand the operation of complex machines. Complex machines are merely combinations of two or more simple machines.

The lever

The simplest machine, and perhaps the one you're most familiar with, is the lever. A seesaw is a familiar example of a lever in which one weight balances the other.

You will find that all levers have three basic parts:

- Fulcrum

- Force or effort

- Resistance

Look at the lever illustration below. You see the pivotal point (fulcrum), the effort, which is applied at a distance from the fulcrum; and a resistance , which acts at a distance from the fulcrum.

Further reading: Physics, High School by Urone, Paul Peter — openstax.org/details/books/physics
Creative Commons Attribution License v4.0

Classes of levers

Levers are classified by the relative positions of the fulcrum, effort and resistance (or load). It is common to call the input force the effort and the **output force** the load or the resistance. This allows the identification of three classes of levers by the relative locations of the fulcrum, the resistance and the effort.

CLASS 1 LEVER

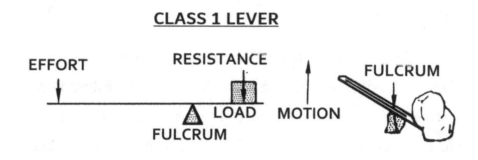

CLASS 2 LEVER

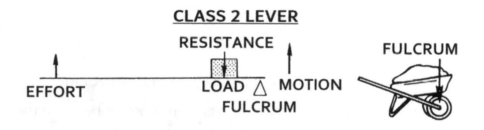

CLASS 3 LEVER

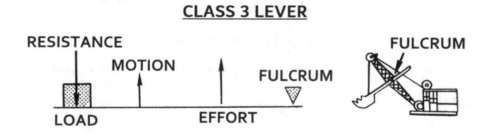

- **Class 1: Fulcrum between the effort and resistance:** the effort is applied on one side of the fulcrum and the resistance (or load) on the

Further reading: Physics, High School by Urone, Paul Peter — openstax.org/details/books/physics

other side, for example, a seesaw, a crowbar or a pair of scissors. Mechanical advantage may be greater than, less than, or equal to 1.

- **Class 2: Resistance (or load) between the effort and fulcrum:** the effort is applied on one side of the resistance and the fulcrum is located on the other side, e.g. in a wheelbarrow, a nutcracker, a bottle opener or the brake pedal of a car, the load arm is smaller than the effort arm, and the mechanical advantage is always greater than one. It is also called force multiplier lever.

- **Class 3: Effort between the fulcrum and resistance:** the resistance (or load) is on one side of the effort and the fulcrum is located on the other side, for example, a pair of tweezers, a hammer, or the jaw. The effort arm is smaller than the load arm. Mechanical advantage is always less than 1. It is also called speed multiplier lever.

Pulleys

A pulley is a wheel on an axle or shaft that is designed to support movement and change of direction of a taut cable or belt, or transfer of power between the shaft and cable or belt. In the case of a pulley supported by a frame or shell that does not transfer power to a shaft, but is used to guide the cable or exert a force, the supporting shell is called a block, and the pulley may be called a sheave.

A pulley may have a groove or grooves between flanges around its circumference to locate the cable or belt. The drive element of a pulley system can be a rope, cable, belt, or chain.

The earliest evidence of pulleys date back to Ancient Egypt in the Twelfth Dynasty.

Further reading: Physics, High School by Urone, Paul Peter — openstax.org/details/books/physics
Creative Commons Attribution License v4.0

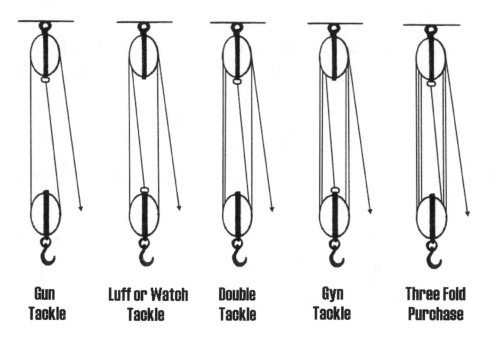

| Gun Tackle | Luff or Watch Tackle | Double Tackle | Gyn Tackle | Three Fold Purchase |

The most important point to remember about block and tackle is that they are simple machines. And simple machines multiply effort or change its direction. You should also remember the following points:

- A pulley is a grooved wheel that turns by the action of a rope in the groove.

- There are different types of pulleys. Pulleys are either fixed or movable.

- You attach a fixed pulley to one place. The fixed pulley helps make work easier by changing the direction of the effort.

- You hook a movable pulley to the object you are lifting. As you pull, the object and the pulley move together. This pulley does not change the direction of the effort, but it does multiply the effort.

- You can use fixed and movable pulleys together to get a large mechanical advantage.

Further reading: Physics, High School by Urone, Paul Peter — openstax.org/details/books/physics
Creative Commons Attribution License v4.0

Wheel and axle

Have you ever tried to open a door when the knob was missing? If you have, you know that trying to twist that small four-sided shaft with your fingers is tough work. That gives you some appreciation of the advantage you get by using a knob. The doorknob is an example of a simple machine called a wheel and axle.

The steering wheel on an automobile, a screwdriver, and a bicycle are all examples of a simple machine. All of these devices use the wheel and axle to multiply the force you exert. If you try to turn a screw with a screwdriver and it doesn't turn, stick a screwdriver bit in the chuck of a brace. The screw will probably go in with little difficulty.

Moment of force

In several situations you can use the wheel-and-axle to speed up motion. The rear-wheel sprocket of a bike, along with the rear wheel itself, is an example. When you are pedaling, the sprocket is attached to the wheel; so the combination is a true wheel-and-axle machine.

Assume that the sprocket has a circumference of 8 inches, and the wheel circumference is 80 inches. If you turn the sprocket at a rate of one revolution per second, each sprocket tooth moves at a speed of 8 inches per second. Since the wheel makes one revolution for each revolution made by the sprocket, any point on the tire must move through a distance of 80 inches in 1 second. So, for every 8-inch movement of a point on the sprocket, you have moved a corresponding point on the wheel through 80 inches.

Since a complete revolution of the sprocket and wheel requires only 1 second, the speed of a point on the circumference of the wheel is 80 inches per second, or ten times the speed of a tooth on the sprocket. (Both sprocket and wheel make the same number of revolutions per second, so the speed of turning for the two is the same.)

Further reading: Physics, High School by Urone, Paul Peter — openstax.org/details/books/physics
Creative Commons Attribution License v4.0

Here's an idea that can help you understand the wheel and axle, as well as other machines. You've probably noticed that the force you apply to a lever starts to turn or rotate it about the fulcrum. And when you turn the steering wheel of a car, it starts to rotate the steering column.

Whenever you use a lever, or a wheel and axle, your effort on the lever arm or the rim of the wheel causes it to rotate about the fulcrum or the axle in one direction or another. If the rotation occurs in the same direction as the hands of a clock, we call that direction clockwise. If the rotation occurs in the opposite direction from that of the hands of a clock, we call that direction of rotation counterclockwise.

The inclined plane and the wedge

You've probably watched a driver load barrels on a truck. He backs the truck up to the curb. The driver then places a long double plank or ramp from the sidewalk to the tailgate, and then rolls the barrel up the ramp. A 32-gallon barrel may weigh close to 300 pounds when full, and it would be quite a job to lift one up into the truck. Actually, the driver is using a simple machine called the inclined plane. You have seen the inclined plane used in many situations. A mountain highway, a cattle ramps, and a gangplank are familiar examples.

The inclined plane permits you to overcome a large resistance, by applying a small force through a longer distance when raising the load. Look at the illustration below.

Further reading: Physics, High School by Urone, Paul Peter — opcnotax.org/details/books/physics
Creative Commons Attribution License v4.0

Here you see a driver easing the 300-pound barrel up to the bed of the truck, three feet above the sidewalk. He is using a plank 9 feet long. If he didn't use the ramp at all, he'd have to apply 300-pound force straight up through the 3-foot distance. With the ramp, he can apply his effort over the entire nine feet of the plank as he rolls the barrel to a height of three feet. He uses a force only three-ninths of 300, or 100 pounds, to do the job.

The screw

The screw is a simple machine that has many uses. The vise on a workbench makes use of the mechanical advantage of the screw. You get the same advantage using glued screw clamps to hold pieces of furniture together, a jack to lift an automobile, or a food processor to grind meat.

A screw is a modification of the inclined plane. Cut a sheet of paper in the shape of a right triangle and you have an inclined plane. Wind this paper around a pencil, as in the illustration below, and you can see that the screw is actually an inclined plane wrapped around a cylinder. As you turn the pencil, the paper is wound up so that its hypotenuse forms a spiral thread. The pitch of the screw and paper is the distance between identical points on the same threads measured along the length of the screw.

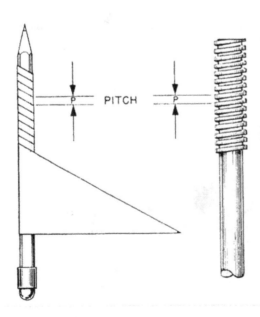

PITCH

Further reading: Physics, High School by Urone, Paul Peter — openstax.org/details/books/physics
Creative Commons Attribution License v4.0

Let's recap the basic information about the screw:

- The screw is a modification of the inclined plane—modified to give you a high mechanical advantage.

- As in all machines, the actual mechanical advantage equals the resistance divided by the effort.

- In many applications of the screw, you make use of the large amount of friction that is commonly present in this simple machine.

- By using the screw, you reduce large amounts of circular motion to very small amounts of straight-line motion.

Gears

Did you ever take a clock apart to see what made it tick? We use gears in many machines. Frequently the gears are hidden from view in a protective case filled with grease or oil, and you may not see them.

An old-fashioned eggbeater gives you a simple demonstration of the three jobs that gears do. They can change the direction of motion, increase or decrease the speed of the applied motion, and magnify or reduce the force that you apply.

Further reading: Physics, High School by Urone, Paul Peter — openstax.org/details/books/physics
Creative Commons Attribution License v4.0

Gears also give you a positive drive. There can be, and usually is, creep or slip in a

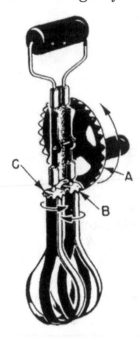

belt drive. However, gear teeth are always in mesh, so there can be no creep and slip. Follow the directional changes in the illustration above. The crank handle turns in the direction shown by the arrow—clockwise—when viewed from the right. The 32 teeth on the large vertical wheel (A) mesh with the 8 teeth on the right-hand horizontal wheel (B), which rotates as shown by the arrow. Notice that as B turns in a clockwise direction, its teeth mesh with those of wheel C and cause wheel C to revolve in the opposite direction.

The rotation of the crank handle has been transmitted by gears to the beater blades, which also rotate. Now figure out how the gears change the speed of motion. There are 32 teeth on gear A and 8 teeth on gear B. However, the gears mesh, so that one complete revolution of A results in four complete revolutions of gear B. And since gears B and C have the same number of teeth, one revolution of B results in one revolution of C. Thus, the blades revolve four times as fast as the crank handle.

At the beginning of this section, we learned that third-class levers increase speed at the expense of force. The same happens with the eggbeater. The magnitude of force changes. The force required to turn the handle is greater than

Further reading: Physics, High School by Urone, Paul Peter — openstax.org/details/books/physics
Creative Commons Attribution License v4.0

the force applied to the frosting by the blades. This results in a mechanical advantage of less than one.

Types of gears

When two shafts are not lying in the same straight line, but are parallel, you can transmit motion from one to the other by spur gears. This setup is shown in the illustration below:

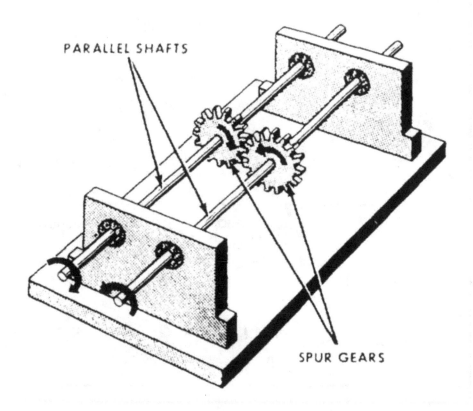

PARALLEL SHAFTS

SPUR GEARS

Spur gears are wheels with mating teeth cut in their surfaces so that one can turn the other without slippage. When the mating teeth are cut so that they are parallel to the axis of rotation, as shown in the illustration, the gears are called straight spur gears.

When two gears of unequal size are meshed together, the smaller of the two is usually called a pinion. By unequal size, we mean an unequal number of teeth

Further reading: Physics, High School by Urone, Paul Peter — openstax.org/details/books/physics
Creative Commons Attribution License v4.0

causing one gear to be a larger diameter than the other. The teeth, themselves, must be of the same size to mesh properly.

The most commonly used gears are the straight spur gears. Often you'll run across another type of spur gear called the helical spur gear. In helical gears the teeth are cut slantwise across the working face of the gear. One end of the tooth, therefore, lies ahead of the other. Thus, each tooth has a leading end and a trailing end. The illustration below shows you the construction of these gears.

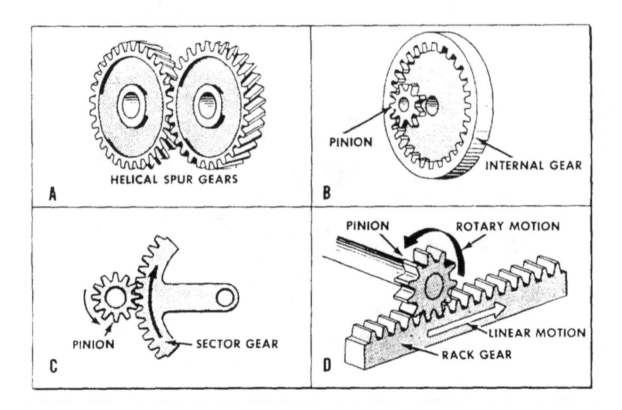

Let's recap what we've learned about gears:

- Gears can do a job for you by changing the direction, speed, or size of the force you apply.

- When two external gears mesh, they always turn in opposite directions. You can make them turn in the same direction by placing an idler gear between the two.

Further reading: Physics, High School by Urone, Paul Peter — openstax.org/details/books/physics
Creative Commons Attribution License v4.0

- The product of the number of teeth on each of the driver gears divided by the product of the number of teeth on each of the driven gears gives you the speed ratio of any gear train.

- The theoretical mechanical advantage of any gear train is the product of the number of teeth on the driven gear wheels, divided by the product of the number of teeth on the driver gears.

- The overall theoretical mechanical advantage of a compound machine is equal to the product of the theoretical mechanical advantages of all the simple machines that make it up.

- We can use cams to change rotary motion into linear motion.

Work

Measurement

You know that machines help you to do work. What is work? Work doesn't mean simply applying a force. Work in the mechanical sense, is done when resistance is overcome by a force acting through a measurable distance.

Work involves two factors-force and movement through a distance. You measure force in pounds and distance in feet. Therefore, you measure work in units called foot-pounds. You do 1 foot-pound of work when you lift a 1-pound weight through a height of 1 foot, You also do one-foot-pound of work when you apply 1 pound of force on any object through a distance of one foot.

Friction

Suppose you are going to push a 400-pound crate up a 12-foot ramp; the upper end is three feet higher than the lower end. You decide that a 100-pound push will do the job. The height you will raise the crate is one-fourth of the distance through which you will exert your push. The theoretical mechanical advantage is four. Then you push on the crate, applying 100 pounds of force; but

Further reading: Physics, High School by Urone, Paul Peter — openstax.org/details/books/physics
Creative Commons Attribution License v4.0

nothing happens! You've forgotten about the friction between the surface of the crate and the surface of the ramp. This friction acts as a resistance to the movement of the crate; you must overcome this resistance to move the crate. In fact, you might have to push as much as 150 pounds to move it. You would use 50 pounds to overcome the frictional resistance, and the remaining 100 pounds would be the useful push that would move the crate up the ramp.

Friction is the resistance that one surface offers to its movement over another surface. The amount of friction depends upon the nature of the two surfaces and the forces that hold them together. In many instances fiction is useful to you. Friction helps you hold back the crate from sliding down the inclined ramp. The cinders you throw under the wheels of your car when it's slipping on an icy pavement increase the friction. You wear rubber-soled shoes in the gym to keep from slipping. Trains carry a supply of sand to drop on the tracks in front of the driving wheels to increase the friction between the wheels and the track. Nails hold structures together because of the friction between the nails and the lumber.

You make friction work for you when you slow up an object in motion, when you want traction, and when you prevent motion from taking place. When you want a machine to run smoothly and at high efficiency, you eliminate as much friction as possible by oiling and greasing bearings and honing and smoothing rubbing surfaces.

Where you apply force to cause motion, friction makes the actual mechanical advantage fall short of the theoretical mechanical advantage. Because of friction, you have to make a greater effort to overcome the resistance that you want to move. If you place a marble and a lump of sugar on a table and give each an equal push, the marble will move farther. That is because rolling friction is always less than sliding friction. You take advantage of this fact whenever you use ball bearings or roller bearings.

Force

Further reading: Physics, High School by Urone, Paul Peter — openstax.org/details/books/physics
Creative Commons Attribution License v4.0

Force is the pull of gravity exerted on an object or an object's thrust of energy against friction. You apply a force on a machine; the machine, in turn, transmits a force to the load. However, other elements besides men and machines can also exert a force. For example, if you've been on a sailboat, you know that the wind can exert a force. Further, after the waves have knocked you on your ear a couple of times, you have grasped the idea that water, too, can exert a force.

Measuring force

Weight is a measurement of the force, or pull of gravity, on an object. You've had a lot of experience in measuring forces. At times, you have estimated or "guessed' the weight of a package you were going to mail by "hefting" it. However, to find its accurate weight, you would have put it on a force-measuring device known as a scale. Scales are of two types: spring and balanced.

Spring scale

You can readily measure force with a spring scale. An Englishman named Hooke invented the spring scale. He discovered that hanging a 1-pound weight on a spring caused the spring to stretch a certain distance and that hanging a two-pound weight on the spring caused it to stretch twice as far. By attaching a pointer to the spring and inserting the pointer through a face, he could mark points on the face to indicate various measurements in pounds and ounces.

We use this type of scale to measure the pull of gravity-the weight-of an object or the force of a pull exerted against friction.

Balanced scale

The problem with the spring-type scale eventually led to the invention of the balanced scale, shown in the illustration below.

Further reading: Physics, High School by Urone, Paul Peter — openstax.org/details/books/physics
Creative Commons Attribution License v4.0

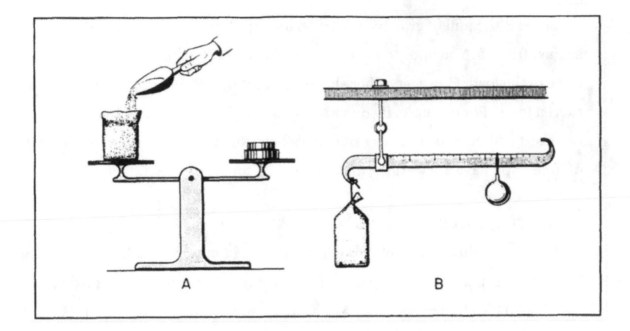

This type of scale is an application of first-class levers. The one on the left is the simplest type. Since the distance from the fulcrum to the center of each platform is equal, the scales balance when equal weights are placed on the platforms. With your knowledge of levers, you can figure out how them scale on the right operates.

Pressure

Pressure is the amount of force within a specific area. You measure air, steam, and gas pressure and the fluid pressure in hydraulic systems in pounds per square inch (psi). However, you measure water pressure in pounds per square foot.

Let's look at how pressure affects your ability to walk across snow. Have you ever tried to walk on freshly fallen snow only to have your feet break through the crust when you put your weight on it? If you had worn snowshoes, you could have walked across the snow without sinking; but do you know why? Snowshoes do not reduce your weight, or the amount of force, exerted on the snow; they merely distribute it over a larger area. In doing that, the snowshoes reduce the pressure per square inch of the force you exert.

Further reading: Physics, High School by Urone, Paul Peter — openstax.org/details/books/physics
Creative Commons Attribution License v4.0

Let's figure out how that works. If a man weighs 160 pounds, that weight, or force, is more or less evenly distributed by the soles of his shoes. The area of the soles of an average man's shoes is roughly 60 square inches. Each of those square inches has to carry 160 ÷ 60= 2.6 pounds of that man's weight. Since 2 to 6 pounds per square inch is too much weight for the snow crest to support, his feet break through.

When the man puts on snowshoes, he distributes his weight over an area of about 900 square inches, depending on the size of the snowshoes. The force on each of those square inches is equal to only 160 ÷ 900 = 0.18 pounds. Therefore, with snowshoes on, he exerts a pressure of 0.18 psi. With this decreased pressure, the snow can easily support him.

Let's recap the main points about force and pressure.

- A force is a push or a pull exerted on or by an object.

- You measure force in pounds.

- Pressure is the force per unit area exerted on an object or exerted by an object. You measure it in pounds per square inch (psi).

- Spring scales and lever balances are familiar instruments you use for measuring forces.

- Pressure is generally relative; that is, it is sometimes greater— sometimes less—than normal air pressure. Pressure that is less than the normal air pressure is called a vacuum.

Physics

Physics is about trying to find the simple laws that describe all natural phenomena.

Further reading: Physics, High School by Urone, Paul Peter — openstax.org/details/books/physics
Creative Commons Attribution License v4.0

Physics operates on a vast range of scales of length, mass, and time. Scientists use the concept of the **order of magnitude** of a number to track which phenomena occur on which scales. They also use orders of magnitude to compare the various scales.

Scientists attempt to describe the world by formulating models, theories, and laws.

Units and Standards

Systems of units are built up from a small number of base units, which are defined by accurate and precise measurements of conventionally chosen base quantities. Other units are then derived as algebraic combinations of the base units.

Two commonly used systems of units are English units and SI units (commonly known as the metric system). All scientists and most of the other people in the world use SI, whereas nonscientists in the United States still tend to use English units.

The SI base units of length, mass, and time are the meter (m), kilogram (kg), and second (s), respectively.

SI units are a metric system of units, meaning values can be calculated by factors of 10. Metric prefixes may be used with metric units to scale the base units to sizes appropriate for almost any application.

Unit Conversion

To convert a quantity from one unit to another, multiply by conversions factors in such a way that you cancel the units you want to get rid of and introduce the units you want to end up with.

Be careful with areas and volumes. Units obey the rules of algebra so, for example, if a unit is squared we need two factors to cancel it.

Further reading: Physics, High School by Urone, Paul Peter — openstax.org/details/books/physics
Creative Commons Attribution License v4.0

Dimensional Analysis

The dimension of a physical quantity is just an expression of the base quantities from which it is derived.

All equations expressing physical laws or principles must be dimensionally consistent. This fact can be used as an aid in remembering physical laws, as a way to check whether claimed relationships between physical quantities are possible, and even to derive new physical laws.

Physics: Newton's first law

According to Newton's first law, there must be a cause for any change in velocity (a change in either magnitude or direction) to occur. This law is also known as the **law of inertia**.

Friction is an external force that causes an object to slow down.

Inertia is the tendency of an object to remain at rest or remain in motion. Inertia is related to an object's mass.

If an object's velocity relative to a given frame is constant, then the frame is inertial. This means that for an inertial reference frame, Newton's first law is valid.

Equilibrium is achieved when the forces on a system are balanced.

A net force of zero means that an object is either at rest or moving with constant velocity; that is, it is not accelerating.

Newton's Second Law

An external force acts on a system from outside the system, as opposed to internal forces, which act between components within the system.

Further reading: Physics, High School by Urone, Paul Peter — openstax.org/details/books/physics
Creative Commons Attribution License v4.0

Newton's second law of motion says that the net external force on an object with a certain mass is directly proportional to and in the same direction as the acceleration of the object.

Newton's second law can also describe net force as the instantaneous rate of change of momentum. Thus, a net external force causes nonzero acceleration.

Mass and Weight

Mass is the quantity of matter in a substance.

The weight of an object is the net force on a falling object, or its gravitational force. The object experiences acceleration due to gravity.

Some upward resistance force from the air acts on all falling objects on Earth, so they can never truly be in free fall.

Careful distinctions must be made between free fall and weightlessness using the definition of weight as force due to gravity acting on an object of a certain mass.

Newton's Third Law

Newton's third law of motion represents a basic symmetry in nature, with an experienced force equal in magnitude and opposite in direction to an exerted force.

Two equal and opposite forces do not cancel because they act on different systems.

Action-reaction pairs include a swimmer pushing off a wall, helicopters creating lift by pushing air down, and an octopus propelling itself forward by ejecting water from its body. Rockets, airplanes, and cars are pushed forward by a thrust reaction force.

Choosing a system is an important analytical step in understanding the physics of a problem and solving it.

Further reading: Physics, High School by Urone, Paul Peter — openstax.org/details/books/physics
Creative Commons Attribution License v4.0

Common Forces

When an object rests on a surface, the surface applies a force to the object that supports the weight of the object. This supporting force acts perpendicular to and away from the surface. It is called a **normal force**.

When an object rests on a nonaccelerating horizontal surface, the magnitude of the normal force is equal to the weight of the object.

When an object rests on an inclined plane that makes an angle θ with the horizontal surface, the weight of the object can be resolved into components that act perpendicular and parallel to the surface of the plane.

The pulling force that acts along a stretched flexible connector, such as a rope or cable, is called tension. When a rope supports the weight of an object at rest, the tension in the rope is equal to the weight of the object. If the object is accelerating, tension is greater than weight, and if it is decelerating, tension is less than weight.

The force of friction is a force experienced by a moving object (or an object that has a tendency to move) parallel to the interface opposing the motion (or its tendency).

The force developed in a spring obeys **Hooke's law**, according to which its magnitude is proportional to the displacement and has a sense in the opposite direction of the displacement.

Real forces have a physical origin, whereas fictitious forces occur because the observer is in an accelerating or noninertial frame of reference.

Solving Problems with Newton's Laws

Newton's laws of motion can be applied in numerous situations to solve motion problems.

Further reading: Physics, High School by Urone, Paul Peter — openstax.org/details/books/physics
Creative Commons Attribution License v4.0

Some problems contain multiple force vectors acting in different directions on an object. Be sure to draw diagrams, resolve all force vectors into horizontal and vertical components, and draw a free-body diagram. Always analyze the direction in which an object accelerates so that you can determine whether Fnet=ma or Fnet=0.

The normal force on an object is not always equal in magnitude to the weight of the object. If an object is accelerating vertically, the normal force is less than or greater than the weight of the object. Also, if the object is on an inclined plane, the normal force is always less than the full weight of the object.

Some problems contain several physical quantities, such as forces, acceleration, velocity, or position. You can apply concepts from **kinematics** and **dynamics** to solve these problems.

Sample ASVAB questions

Here are some examples of the sort of questions you'll see on ASVAB subtests.

Remember, you have access to several full-length practice tests at ASVABcram.com.

1. What type of gear system is pictured below?

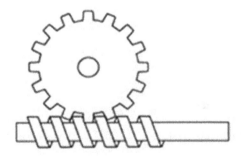

a. Spiral Gear

Further reading: Physics, High School by Urone, Paul Peter — openstax.org/details/books/physics
Creative Commons Attribution License v4.0

b. Bevel Gear

c. Worm Gear

d. Rack and Pinion

(Correct answer is d, Rack and Pinion)

2. What procedure is used to enlarge a hole?

a. Reaming

b. Drilling

c. Boring

d. Thread Cutting

(Correct answer is c, Boring.)

3. What tool is pictured below?

Further reading: Physics, High School by Urone, Paul Peter — openstax.org/details/books/physics
Creative Commons Attribution License v4.0

a. Compass

b. Micrometer

c. Circular Wrench

d. Protractor

(Correct answer is a, Compass.)

4. What does the illustration below represent?

Further reading: Physics, High School by Urone, Paul Peter — openstax.org/details/books/physics
Creative Commons Attribution License v4.0

a. Horizontal Scale

b. Knife Design

c. Airfoil

d. Center of Gravity

(Correct answer is c, Airfoil.)

.

Further reading: Physics, High School by Urone, Paul Peter — openstax.org/details/books/physics
Creative Commons Attribution License v4.0

► ELECTRONICS INFORMATION

Electronics is another area of the ASVAB that will help you qualify for certain technical jobs, but it doesn't contribute to your AFQT score. Electronics technicians in each of the services repair and maintain some of the most sophisticated equipment anywhere. Cyber operations, electronic warfare, cryptography, radar, and missile systems are just a few of the opportunities available to service members with an aptitude in electronics.

Exactly what is electricity? It's defined as "the flow of electrons through simple materials and devices" or "that force which moves electrons." Scientists think electricity is produced by very tiny particles called electrons and protons. These particles are too small to be seen, but exist as subatomic particles in the atom. To understand how they exist, you must first understand the structure of the atom.

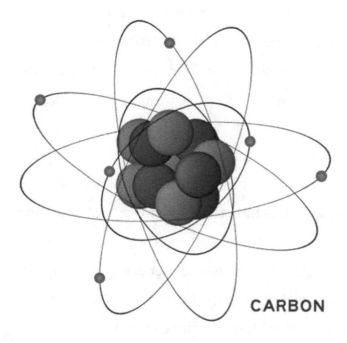

CARBON

The atom

Elements are the basic blocks of all matter. The atom is the smallest particle to which an element can be reduced while still keeping the properties of that element. An atom consists of a positively charged nucleus surrounded by negatively charged electrons, so that the atom as a whole is electrically neutral. The nucleus is composed of two kinds of subatomic particles, protons and neutrons, as shown above. The proton carries a single unit positive charge equal in magnitude to the electron charge. The neutron is slightly heavier than the proton and is electrically neutral, as the name implies. These two particles exist in various combinations, depending upon the element involved. The electron is the fundamental negative charge (-) of electricity and revolves around the nucleus, or center, of the atom in concentric orbits, or shells.

The proton is the fundamental positive charge of electricity and is located in the nucleus. The number of protons in the nucleus of any atom specifies the atomic number of that atom or of that element. For example, the carbon atom contains six protons in its nucleus; therefore, the atomic number for carbon is six. In its natural state, an atom of any element contains an equal number of electrons and protons. The negative charge (-) of each electron is equal in magnitude to the positive charge (+) of each proton; therefore, the two opposite charges cancel, and the atom is said to be electrically neutral, or in balance.

Electrostatic force

One of the mysteries of the atom is that the electron and the nucleus attract each other. This attraction is called electrostatic force, the force that holds the electron in orbit. Without this electrostatic force, the electron, which is traveling at high speed, could not stay in its orbit. Bodies that attract each other in this way are called charged bodies. As mentioned previously, the electron has a negative charge, and the nucleus (due to the proton) has a positive charge.

Further Reading: Physics, High School by Urone, Paul Peter — openstax.org/details/books/physics
Creative Commons Attribution License v4.0

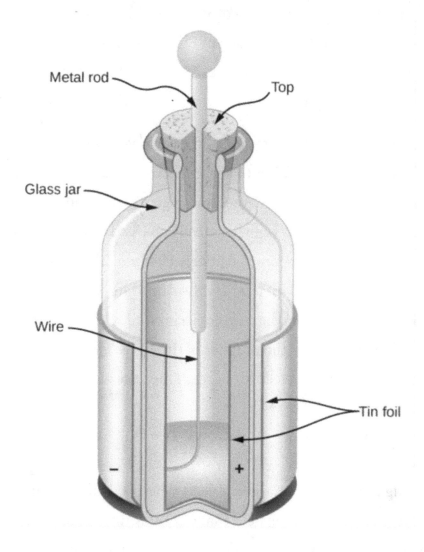

Above: A Leyden jar (an early version of what is now called a capacitor) allowed experimenters to store large amounts of electrical charge. Benjamin Franklin used such a jar to demonstrate that lightning behaved exactly like the electricity he got from the equipment in his laboratory.

The First Law of Electrostatics

The negative charge of the electron is equal, but opposite to, the positive charge of the proton.

Further Reading: Physics, High School by Urone, Paul Peter — openstax.org/details/books/physics
Creative Commons Attribution License v4.0

These charges are referred to as electrostatic charges. In nature, **unlike** charges (like electrons and protons) attract each other, and **like charges** repel each other. These facts are known as the First Law of Electrostatics and are sometimes referred to as the law of electrical charges. This law should be remembered because it is one of the vital concepts in electricity.

Some atoms can lose electrons and others can gain electrons; thus, it is possible to transfer electrons from one object to another. When this occurs, the equal distribution of negative and positive charges no longer exists. One object will contain an excess of electrons and become negatively charged, and the other will become deficient in electrons and become positively charged. These objects, which can contain billions of atoms, will then follow the same law of electrostatics as the electron and proton. The electrons that can move around within an object are said to be free electrons. The greater the number of these free electrons an object contains, the greater its negative electric charge. Thus, the electric charge can be used as a measure of electrons.

Electrostatic Field

A special force is acting between the charged objects discussed above. Forces of this type are the result of an electrostatic field that exists around each charged particle or object. This electrostatic field, and the force it creates, can be illustrated with lines called "lines of force" as shown below.

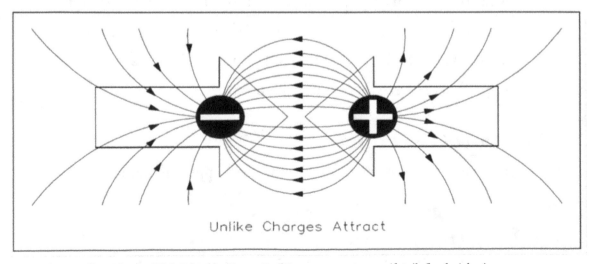

Unlike Charges Attract

Further Reading: Physics, High School by Urone, Paul Peter — openstax.org/details/books/physics
Creative Commons Attribution License v4.0

Charged objects repel or attract each other because of the way these fields act together. This force is present with every charged object. When two objects of opposite charge are brought near one another, the electrostatic field is concentrated in the area between them. The direction of the small arrows shows the direction of the force as it would act upon an electron if it were released into the electric field.

The strength of the attraction or of the repulsion force depends upon two factors:

(1) the amount of charge on each object, and

(2) the distance between the objects.

The greater the charge on the objects, the greater the electrostatic field. The greater the distance between the objects, the weaker the electrostatic field between them, and vice versa. This leads us to the law of electrostatic attraction, commonly referred to as Coulomb's Law of electrostatic charges, which states that the force of electrostatic attraction, or repulsion, is directly proportional to the product of the two charges and inversely proportional to the square of the distance between them as shown below.

$$F = K\frac{q_1 \cdot q_2}{d^2}$$

where

F	= force of electrostatic attraction or prepulsion (Newtons)
K	= constant of proportionality (Coulomb ^{2}/N-m^2)
q_1	= charge of first particle (Coulombs)
q_2	= charge of second particle (Coulombs)
d	= distance between two particles (Meters)

Free Electrons

Electrons are in rapid motion around the nucleus. While the electrostatic force is trying to pull the nucleus and the electron together, the electron is in

Further Reading: Physics, High School by Urone, Paul Peter — openstax.org/details/books/physics
Creative Commons Attribution License v4.0

motion and trying to pull away. These two effects balance, keeping the electron in orbit. The electrons in an atom exist in different energy levels. The energy level of an electron is proportional to its distance from the nucleus.

Higher energy level electrons exist in orbits, or shells, that are farther away from the nucleus. These shells nest inside one another and surround the nucleus. The nucleus is the center of all the shells. The shells are lettered beginning with the shell nearest the nucleus: K, L, M, N, O, P, and Q. Each shell has a maximum number of electrons it can hold. For example, the K shell will hold a maximum of two electrons and the L shell will hold a maximum of eight electrons.

Conductors

Conductors are materials with electrons that are loosely bound to their atoms, or materials that permit free motion of a large number of electrons. Atoms with only one valence electron, such as copper, silver, and gold, are examples of good conductors. Most metals are good conductors.

Insulators

Insulators, or nonconductors, are materials with electrons that are tightly bound to their atoms and require large amounts of energy to free them from the influence of the nucleus. The atoms of good insulators have their valence shells filled with eight electrons, which means they are more than half filled. Any energy applied to such an atom will be distributed among a relatively large number of electrons. Examples of insulators are rubber, plastics, glass, and dry wood.

Further Reading: Physics, High School by Urone, Paul Peter — openstax.org/details/books/physics
Creative Commons Attribution License v4.0

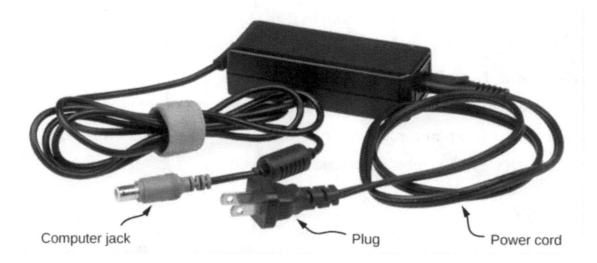

Computer jack   Plug   Power cord

Above: this power adapter uses metal wires and connectors to conduct electricity from the wall socket to a laptop computer. The connecting wires allow electrons to move freely through the cables, which are shielded by rubber and plastic. These materials act as insulators that don't allow electric charge to escape outward.

Resistors

Resistors are made of materials that conduct electricity, but offer opposition to current flow. These types of materials are also called semiconductors because they are neither good conductors nor good insulators. Semiconductors have more than one or two electrons in their valence shells, but less than seven or eight. Examples of semiconductors are carbon, silicon, germanium, tin, and lead. Each has four valence electrons.

Voltage

The basic unit of measure for potential difference is the **volt** (symbol V), and, because the volt unit is used, potential difference is called voltage. An object's electrical charge is determined by the number of electrons that the object has gained or lost. Because such a large number of electrons move, a unit called the **coulomb** is used to indicate the charge. One coulomb is equal to 6.28×10^{18}

Further Reading: Physics, High School by Urone, Paul Peter — openstax.org/details/books/physics
Creative Commons Attribution License v4.0

(billion, billion) electrons. For example, if an object gains one coulomb of negative charge, it has gained 6,280,000,000,000,000,000 extra electrons. A volt is defined as a difference of potential causing one coulomb of current to do one joule of work. A volt is also defined as that amount of force required to force one ampere of current through one ohm of resistance. The latter is the definition with which we will be most concerned in this module.

Current

The density of the atoms in copper wire is such that the valence orbits of the individual atoms overlap, causing the electrons to move easily from one atom to the next. Free electrons can drift from one orbit to another in a random direction. When a potential difference is applied, the direction of their movement is controlled. The strength of the potential difference applied at each end of the wire determines how many electrons change from a random motion to a more directional path through the wire. The movement or flow of these electrons is called electron current flow or just current.

To produce current, the electrons must be moved by a potential difference. The symbol for current is (I). The basic measurement for current is the ampere (A). One ampere of current is defined as the movement of one coulomb of charge past any given point of a conductor during one second of time.

If a copper wire is placed between two charged objects that have a potential difference, all of the negatively-charged free electrons will feel a force pushing

them from the negative charge to the positive charge. This force opposite to the conventional direction of the electrostatic lines of force is shown below.

Further Reading: Physics, High School by Urone, Paul Peter — openstax.org/details/books/physics
Creative Commons Attribution License v4.0

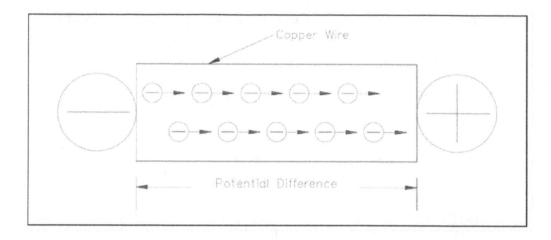

The direction of electron flow is from the negative (-) side of the battery, through the wire, and back to the positive (+) side of the battery. The direction of electron flow is from a point of negative potential to a point of positive potential. The solid arrow shown above indicates the direction of electron flow. As electrons vacate their atoms during electron current flow, positively charged atoms (holes) result. The flow of electrons in one direction causes a flow of positive charges. The direction of the positive charges is in the opposite direction of the electron flow. This flow of positive charges is known as **conventional current**. All of the electrical effects of electron flow from negative to positive, or from a higher potential to a lower potential, are the same as those that would be created by a flow of positive charges in the opposite direction. Therefore, it's important to realize that both conventions are in use and that they are essentially equivalent; that is, all effects predicted are the same.

Generally, electric current flow can be classified as one of two general types: **Direct Current** (DC) or **Alternating Current** (AC). A direct current flows continuously in the same direction. An alternating current periodically reverses direction. An example of DC current is that current obtained from a battery. An example of AC current is common household current.

Real and Ideal Sources

An ideal source is a theoretical concept of an electric current or voltage supply (such as a battery) that has no losses and is a perfect voltage or current supply.

Further Reading: Physics, High School by Urone, Paul Peter — openstax.org/details/books/physics
Creative Commons Attribution License v4.0

Ideal sources are used for analytical purposes only since they cannot occur in nature.

A real source is a real life current or voltage supply that has some losses associated with it.

Terminology Summary

- Conductor - material with electrons loosely bound to its atoms or that permits free motion of large number of electrons

- Insulator - material with electrons tightly bound to its atoms; requires large amounts of energy to free electrons from its nuclei

- Resistor - material that conducts electricity, but opposes current flow

- Electron Current Flow - current flow from negative to positive potentials

- Conventional Current Flow - current flow from positive to negative potentials

- Direct Current - current flow continuously in the same direction

- Alternating Current - current flow periodically reverses direction

- Ideal Source - theoretical current or voltage supply with no losses

- Real Source - actual current or voltage supply with losses

System Internationale (SI) Metric System

Electrical units of measurement are based on the International (metric) System, also known as the SI System that we mentioned previously. Units of electrical measurement include the following:

- Ampere

- Volt

- Ohm

- Siemens

Further Reading: Physics, High School by Urone, Paul Peter — openstax.org/details/books/physics
Creative Commons Attribution License v4.0

- Watt

- Henry

- Farad

Voltage

Voltage, electromotive force (emf), or potential difference, is described as the pressure or force that causes electrons to move in a conductor. In electrical formulas and equations, you will see voltage symbolized with a capital E, while on laboratory equipment or schematic diagrams, the voltage is often represented with a capital V.

Current

Electron current, or amperage, is described as the movement of free electrons through a conductor. In electrical formulas, current is symbolized with a capital I, while in the laboratory or on schematic diagrams, it is common to use a capital A to indicate amps or amperage (amps).

Resistance

Now that we have discussed the concepts of voltage and current, we are ready to discuss a third key concept called resistance. Resistance is defined as the opposition to current flow. The amount of opposition to current flow produced by a material depends upon the amount of available free electrons it contains and the types of obstacles the electrons encounter as they attempt to move through the material. Resistance is measured in **ohms** and is represented by the symbol (R) in equations. One ohm is defined as that amount of resistance that will limit the current in a conductor to one ampere when the potential difference (voltage) applied to the conductor is one volt. The shorthand notation for ohm is the Greek letter capital omega, Ω. If a voltage is applied to a conductor, current flows. The amount of current flow depends upon the resistance of the conductor. The lower

Further Reading: Physics, High School by Urone, Paul Peter — openstax.org/details/books/physics
Creative Commons Attribution License v4.0

the resistance, the higher the current flow for a given amount of voltage. The higher the resistance, the lower the current flow.

Ohm's Law

In 1827, George Simon Ohm discovered that there was a definite relationship between voltage, current, and resistance in an electrical circuit.

Ohm's Law states that the current through a conductor between two points is directly proportional to the voltage across the two points. Introducing the constant of proportionality, the resistance, one arrives at the usual mathematical equation that describes this relationship, where I is the current through the conductor in units of amperes, V is the voltage measured across the conductor in units of volts, and R is the resistance of the conductor in units of ohms.

Ohm's Law

$$I = \frac{V}{R}$$

Electric current = Voltage / Resistance

More specifically, Ohm's law states that the R in this relation is constant, independent of the current.

Conductance

The word "reciprocal" is sometimes used to mean "the opposite of." The opposite, or reciprocal, of resistance is called conductance. As described above, resistance is the opposition to current flow. Since resistance and conductance are opposites, conductance can be defined as the ability to conduct current. For example, if a wire has a high conductance, it will have low resistance, and vice-versa. Conductance is found by taking the reciprocal of the resistance.

Further Reading: Physics, High School by Urone, Paul Peter — openstax.org/details/books/physics
Creative Commons Attribution License v4.0

The unit used to specify conductance is called mho, which is ohm spelled backwards. The symbol for "mho" is the Greek letter omega inverted, ℧ .

Power

Electricity is generally used to do some sort of work, such as turning a motor or generating heat. Specifically, power is the rate at which work is done, or the rate at which heat is generated. The unit commonly used to specify electric power is the watt. In equations, you will find power abbreviated with the capital letter P, and watts, the units of measure for power, are abbreviated with the capital letter W. Power is also described as the current (I) in a circuit times the voltage (E) across the circuit.

Inductance

Inductance is defined as the ability of a coil to store energy, induce a voltage in itself, and oppose changes in current flowing through it. The symbol used to indicate inductance in electrical formulas and equations is a capital L. The units of measurement are called henries.

The unit henry is abbreviated by using the capital letter H. One henry is the amount of inductance (L) that permits one volt to be induced (VL) when the current through the coil changes at a rate of one ampere per second.

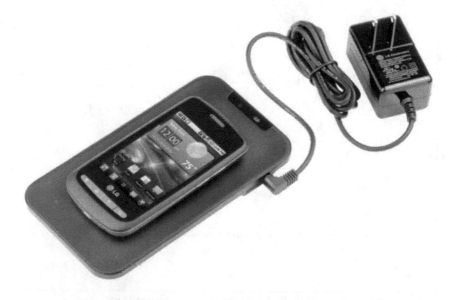

Further Reading: Physics, High School by Urone, Paul Peter — openstax.org/details/books/physics
Creative Commons Attribution License v4.0

Above: A smartphone charging mat contains a coil that receives alternating current, or current that is constantly increasing and decreasing. The varying current induces an emf in the smartphone, which charges its battery. The black box containing the electrical plug also contains a transformer that modifies the current from the outlet to suit the needs of the smartphone.

Capacitance

Capacitance is defined as the ability to store an electric charge and is symbolized by the capital letter C. Capacitance (C), measured in farads, is equal to the amount of charge (Q) that can be stored in a device or capacitor divided by the voltage (E) applied across the device or capacitor plates when the charge was stored.

Capacitors are important components of electrical circuits in many electronic devices, including pacemakers, cell phones, and computers.

Electrical Units Summary

Parameter	Measuring Unit	Relationship
Voltage	volt (V or E)	$E = I \times R$
Current	amp (I)	$I = \dfrac{E}{R}$
Resistance	ohm (R or Ω)	$R = \dfrac{E}{I}$
Conductance	mho (G or ℧)	$G = \dfrac{I}{R} = \dfrac{I}{E}$
Power	watt (W)	$P = I \times E$ or $P = I^2 R$
Inductance	henry (L or H)	$V_L = -L\left(\dfrac{\Delta I}{\Delta t}\right)$
Capacitance	farad (C)	$C = \dfrac{Q}{E}$ (Q = charge)

Further Reading: Physics, High School by Urone, Paul Peter — openstax.org/details/books/physics

Methods of producing voltage (electricity)

This section provides information on the following methods of producing electricity:

- Electrochemistry

- Static (friction)

- Induction (magnetism)

- Piezoclectric (pressure)

- Thermal (heat)

- Light

- Thermionic emission

Electrochemistry

Chemicals can be combined with certain metals to cause a chemical reaction that will transfer electrons to produce electrical energy. This process works on the electrochemistry principle.

One example of this principle is the voltaic chemical cell. A chemical reaction produces and maintains opposite charges on two dissimilar metals that serve as the positive and negative terminals. The metals are in contact with an electrolyte solution. Connecting together more than one of these cells will produce a battery.

Static Electricity

Atoms with the proper number of electrons in orbit around them are in a neutral state, or have a **zero charge**. A body of matter consisting of these atoms will neither attract nor repel other matter that is in its vicinity. If electrons are removed from the atoms in this body of matter, as happens due to friction when

Further Reading: Physics, High School by Urone, Paul Peter — openstax.org/details/books/physics
Creative Commons Attribution License v4.0

one rubs a glass rod with a silk cloth, it will become electrically positive. If this body of matter (e.g., glass rod) comes near, but not in contact with, another body having a normal charge, an electric force is exerted between them because of their unequal charges. The existence of this force is referred to as static electricity or electrostatic force.

Example:

Have you ever walked across a carpet and received a shock when you touched a metal door knob? This happened because your shoe soles built up a charge by rubbing on the carpet, and this charge was transferred to your body. Your body became positively charged and, when you touched the zero-charged door knob, electrons were transferred to your body until both you and the door knob had equal charges.

Magnetic Induction

A generator is a machine that converts mechanical energy into electrical energy by using the principle of magnetic induction. Magnetic induction is used to produce a voltage by rotating coils of wire through a stationary magnetic field or by rotating a magnetic field through stationary coils of wire. This is one of the most useful and widely employed applications of producing vast quantities of electric power.

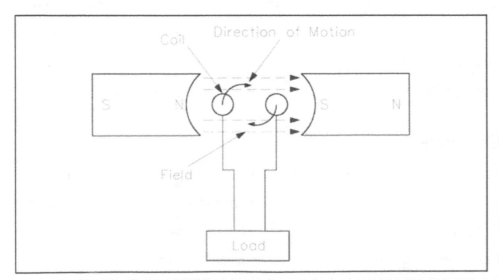

Further Reading: Physics, High School by Urone, Paul Peter — openstax.org/details/books/physics
Creative Commons Attribution License v4.0

Piezoelectric Effect

By applying pressure to certain crystals (such as quartz or Rochelle salts) or certain ceramics (like barium titanate), electrons can be driven out of orbit in the direction of the force. Electrons leave one side of the material and accumulate on the other side, building up positive and negative charges on opposite sides. When the pressure is released, the electrons return to their orbits. Some materials will react to bending pressure, while others will respond to twisting pressure. This generation of voltage is known as the **piezoelectric effect**. If external wires are connected while pressure and voltage are present, electrons will flow and current will be produced. If the pressure is held constant, the current will flow until the potential difference is equalized.

When the force is removed, the material is decompressed and immediately causes an electric force in the opposite direction. The power capacity of these materials is extremely small. However, these materials are very useful because of their extreme sensitivity to changes of mechanical force.

Thermoelectricity

Some materials readily give up their electrons and others readily accept electrons. For example, when two dissimilar metals like copper and zinc are joined together, a transfer of electrons can take place. Electrons will leave the copper atoms and enter the zinc atoms. The zinc gets a surplus of electrons and becomes negatively charged. The copper loses electrons and takes on a positive charge. This creates a voltage potential across the junction of the two metals. The heat energy of normal room temperature is enough to make them release and gain electrons, causing a measurable voltage potential. As more heat energy is applied to the junction, more electrons are released, and the voltage potential becomes greater. When heat is removed and the junction cools, the charges will dissipate and the voltage potential will decrease. This process is called **thermoelectricity**. A device like this is generally referred to as a "thermocouple."

Further Reading: Physics, High School by Urone, Paul Peter — openstax.org/details/books/physics
Creative Commons Attribution License v4.0

The thermoelectric voltage in a thermocouple is dependent upon the heat energy applied to the junction of the two dissimilar metals. Thermocouples are widely used to measure temperature and as heat-sensing devices in automatic temperature controlled equipment.

Photoelectric Effect

Light is a form of energy consisting of small particles of energy called photons. When the photons in a light beam strike the surface of a material, they release their energy and transfer it to the atomic electrons of the material. This energy transfer may dislodge electrons from their orbits around the surface of the substance. Upon losing electrons, the photosensitive (light sensitive) material becomes positively charged and an electric force is created, as shown below.

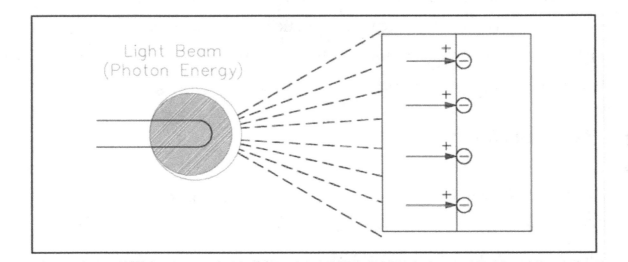

This phenomenon is called the photoelectric effect and has wide applications in electronics, such as photoelectric cells, photovoltaic cells, optical couplers, and television camera tubes. Three uses of the photoelectric effect are described below.

- **Photovoltaic:** The light energy in one of two plates that are joined together causes one plate to release electrons to the other. The plates build up opposite charges, like a battery.

Further Reading: Physics, High School by Urone, Paul Peter — openstax.org/details/books/physics
Creative Commons Attribution License v4.0

- **Photoemission:** The photon energy from a beam of light could cause a surface to release electrons in a vacuum tube. A plate would then collect the electrons.

- **Photoconduction:** The light energy applied to some materials that are normally poor conductors causes free electrons to be produced in the materials so that they become better conductors.

- **Thermionic Emission:** A thermionic energy converter is a device consisting of two electrodes placed near one another in a vacuum. One electrode is normally called the cathode, or emitter, and the other is called the anode, or plate. Ordinarily, electrons in the cathode are prevented from escaping from the surface by a potential-energy barrier. When an electron starts to move away from the surface it induces a corresponding positive charge in the material, which tends to pull it back into the surface. To escape, the electron must somehow acquire enough energy to overcome this energy barrier. At ordinary temperatures, almost none of the electrons can acquire enough energy to escape. However, when the cathode is very hot, the electron energies are greatly increased by thermal motion. At sufficiently high temperatures, a considerable number of electrons are able to escape. The liberation of electrons from a hot surface is called thermionic emission.

The electrons that have escaped from the hot cathode form a cloud of negative charges near it called a space charge. If the plate is maintained positive with respect to the cathode by a battery, the electrons in the cloud are attracted to it. As long as the potential difference between the electrodes is maintained, there will be a steady current flow from the cathode to the plate.

The simplest example of a thermionic device is a vacuum tube diode in which the only electrodes are the cathode and plate, or anode. The diode can be used to convert alternating current (AC) flow to a pulsating direct current (DC) flow.

Further Reading: Physics, High School by Urone, Paul Peter — openstax.org/details/books/physics
Creative Commons Attribution License v4.0

Batteries

A battery consists of two or more chemical cells connected in series. The combination of materials within a battery is used for the purpose of converting chemical energy into electrical energy. To understand how a battery works, we must first discuss the chemical cell. The chemical cell is composed of two electrodes made of different types of metal or metallic compounds which are immersed in an **electrolyte solution**. The chemical actions which result are complicated, and they vary with the type of material used in cell construction. Some knowledge of the basic action of a simple cell will be helpful in understanding the operation of a chemical cell in general.

In the cell, electrolyte ionizes to produce positive and negative ions. Simultaneously, chemical action causes the atoms within one of the electrodes to ionize. Due to this action, electrons are deposited on the electrode, and positive ions from the electrode pass into the electrolyte solution. This causes a negative charge on the electrode and leaves a positive charge in the area near the electrode.

The positive ions, which were produced by ionization of the electrolyte, are repelled to the other electrode. At this electrode, these ions will combine with the electrons. Because this action causes removal of electrons from the electrode, it becomes positively charged.

Rectifiers

Most electrical power generating stations produce alternating current. The major reason for generating AC is that it can be transferred over long distances with fewer losses than DC; however, many of the devices which are used today operate only, or more efficiently, with DC.

For example, transistors, electron tubes, and certain electronic control devices require DC for operation. If we are to operate these devices from ordinary AC outlet receptacles, they must be equipped with rectifier units to convert AC to DC.

Further Reading: Physics, High School by Urone, Paul Peter — openstax.org/details/books/physics
Creative Commons Attribution License v4.0

In order to accomplish this conversion, we use diodes in rectifier circuits. The purpose of a rectifier circuit is to convert AC power to DC.

The most common type of solid state diode rectifier is made of silicon. The diode acts as a gate, which allows current to pass in one direction and blocks current in the other direction. The polarity of the applied voltage determines if the diode will conduct. The two polarities are known as forward bias and reverse bias.

Schematic Diagram

Schematic diagrams are the standard means by which we communicate information in electrical and electronics circuits. On schematic diagrams, the component parts are represented by graphic symbols. Because graphic symbols are small, it is possible to have diagrams in a compact form. The symbols and associated lines show how circuit components are connected and the relationship of those components with one another.

Electric Circuit

Each electrical circuit has at least four basic parts:

(1) a source of electromotive force,

(2) conductors,

(3) load or loads, and

(4) some means of control.

The source of EMF is the battery; the conductors are wires which connect the various component parts; the resistor is the load; and a switch is used as the circuit control device.

Further Reading: Physics, High School by Urone, Paul Peter — openstax.org/details/books/physics
Creative Commons Attribution License v4.0

A **closed circuit** is an uninterrupted, or unbroken, path for current from the source (EMF), through the load, and back to the source.

An **open circuit**, or incomplete circuit, exists if a break in the circuit occurs; this prevents a complete path for current flow.

A **short circuit** is a circuit which offers very little resistance to current flow and can cause dangerously high current flow through a circuit. Short circuits are usually caused by an inadvertent connection between two points in a circuit which offers little or no resistance to current flow.

Series Circuit

A series circuit is a circuit where there is only one path for current flow. In a series circuit the current will be the same throughout the circuit. This means that the current flow through R1 is the same as the current flow through R2 and R3.

Parallel Circuit

Parallel circuits are those circuits which have two or more components connected across the same voltage source. Each parallel path is a branch with its own individual current.

Further Reading: Physics, High School by Urone, Paul Peter — openstax.org/details/books/physics
Creative Commons Attribution License v4.0

Voltage polarity and current direction

Conventional and Electron Flow

The direction of electron flow is from a point of negative potential to a point of positive potential. The direction of positive charges, or holes, is in the opposite direction of electron flow. This flow of positive charges is known as conventional flow. All of the electrical effects of electron flow from negative to positive, or from a high potential to a lower potential, are the same as those that would be created by flow of positive charges in the opposite direction; therefore, it is important to realize that both conventions are in use, and they are essentially equivalent.

Polarities

All voltages and currents have polarity as well as magnitude. In a series circuit, there is only one current, and its polarity is from the negative battery terminal through the rest of the circuit to the positive battery terminal. Voltage drops across loads also have polarities. The easiest way to find these polarities is to use the direction of the electron current as a basis. Then, where the electron current enters the load, the voltage is negative. This holds true regardless of the number or type of loads in the circuit. The drop across the load is opposite to that of the source. The voltage drops oppose the source voltage and reduce it for the other loads. This is because each load uses energy, leaving less energy for other loads.

Kirchhoff's Laws

In all of the circuits examined so far, Ohm's Law described the relationship between current, voltage, and resistance. These circuits have been relatively simple in nature. Many circuits are extremely complex and cannot be solved with Ohm's Law. These circuits have many power sources and branches which would make the use of Ohm's Law impractical or impossible.

Further Reading: Physics, High School by Urone, Paul Peter — openstax.org/details/books/physics
Creative Commons Attribution License v4.0

Through experimentation in 1857 the German physicist Gustav Kirchhoff developed methods to solve complex circuits. Kirchhoff developed two conclusions, known today as **Kirchhoff's Laws**.

- **Law 1:** The sum of the voltage drops around a closed loop is equal to the sum of the voltage sources of that loop (Kirchhoff's Voltage Law).

- **Law 2:** The current arriving at any junction point in a circuit is equal to the current leaving that junction (Kirchhoff's Current Law).

Kirchhoff's two laws may seem obvious based on what we already know about circuit theory. Even though they may seem very simple, they are powerful tools in solving complex and difficult circuits.

Kirchhoff's laws can be related to conservation of energy and charge if we look at a circuit with one load and source. Since all of the power provided from the source is consumed by the load, energy and charge are conserved. Since

voltage and current can be related to energy and charge, then Kirchhoff's laws are only restating the laws governing energy and charge conservation.

The mathematics involved becomes more difficult as the circuits become more complex. Therefore, the discussion here will be limited to solving only relatively simple circuits.

Kirchhoff's first law is also known as his "voltage law." The voltage law gives the relationship between the "voltage drops" around any closed loop in a circuit, and the voltage sources in that loop. The total of these two quantities is always equal.

Kirchhoff's second law is called his current law and states: "At any junction point in a circuit, the current arriving is equal to the current leaving." Thus, if 15 amperes of current arrives at a junction that has two paths leading away from it, 15 amperes will divide among the two branches, but a total of 15 amperes must leave the junction.

Further Reading: Physics, High School by Urone, Paul Peter — openstax.org/details/books/physics
Creative Commons Attribution License v4.0

DC circuit analysis

All of the rules governing DC circuits that have been discussed so far can now be applied to analyze complex DC circuits. To apply these rules effectively, loop equations, node equations, and equivalent resistances must be used.

Loop Equations

As we have already learned, Kirchhoff's Laws provide a practical means to solve for unknowns in a circuit. Kirchhoff's current law states that at any junction point in a circuit, the current arriving is equal to the current leaving. In a series circuit the current is the same at all points in that circuit. In parallel circuits, the total current is equal to the sum of the currents in each branch. Kirchhoff's voltage law states that the sum of all potential differences in closed loop equals zero.

Using Kirchhoff's laws, it is possible to take a circuit with two loops and several power sources and determine loop equations, solve loop currents, and solve individual element currents.

DC circuit faults

Faults within a DC circuit will cause various effects, depending upon the nature of the fault. An understanding of the effects of these faults is necessary to fully understand DC circuit operation.

Open circuit (Series)

A circuit must have a "complete" path for current flow, that is, from the negative side to the positive side of a power source. A series circuit has only one path for current to flow. If this path is broken, no current flows, and the circuit becomes an open circuit.

Further Reading: Physics, High School by Urone, Paul Peter — openstax.org/details/books/physics
Creative Commons Attribution License v4.0

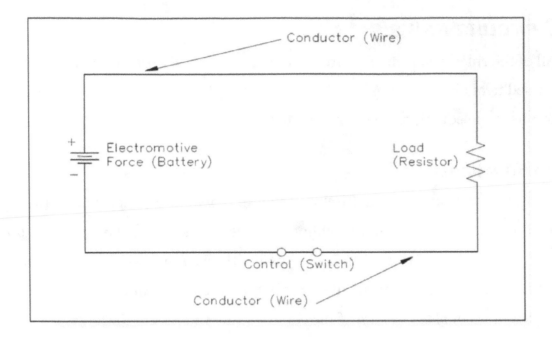

Circuits can be opened deliberately, such as by the use of a switch, or they may be opened by a defect, such as a broken wire or a burned-out resistor.

Since no current flows in an open series circuit, there are no voltage drops across the loads. No power is consumed by the loads, and total power consumed by the circuit is zero.

Open circuit (Parallel)

A parallel circuit has more than one path for current to flow. If one of the paths is opened, current will continue to flow as long as a complete path is provided by one or more of the remaining paths. It does not mean that you cannot stop current flow through a parallel circuit by opening it at one point; it means that the behavior of a parallel circuit depends on where the opening occurs.

Short circuit (Series)

In a DC circuit, the only current limit is the circuit resistance. If there is no resistance in a circuit, or if the resistance suddenly becomes zero, a very large current will flow. This condition of very low resistance and high current flow is known as a "short circuit." A short circuit is said to exist if the circuit resistance is

Further Reading: Physics, High School by Urone, Paul Peter — openstax.org/details/books/physics
Creative Commons Attribution License v4.0

so low that current increases to a point where damage can occur to circuit components. With an increase in circuit current flow, the terminal voltage of the energy source will decrease. This occurs due to the internal resistance of the energy source causing an increased voltage drop within the energy source. The increased current flow resulting from a short circuit can damage power sources, burn insulation, and start fires. Fuses are provided in circuits to protect against short circuits.

Short circuit (Parallel)

When a parallel circuit becomes short circuited, the same effect occurs as in a series circuit: there is a sudden and very large increase in circuit current. Parallel circuits are more likely than series circuits to develop damaging short circuits. This is because each load is connected directly across the power source. If any of the load becomes shorted, the resistance between the power source terminals is practically zero. If a series load becomes shorted, the resistance of the other loads keeps the circuit resistance from dropping to zero.

Terms to remember:

charging by induction

process by which an electrically charged object brought near a neutral object creates a charge separation in that object

conduction electron

electron that is free to move away from its atomic orbit

conductor

material that allows electrons to move separately from their atomic orbits; object with properties that allow charges to move about freely within it

continuous charge distribution

Further Reading: Physics, High School by Urone, Paul Peter — openstax.org/details/books/physics
Creative Commons Attribution License v4.0

total source charge composed of so large a number of elementary charges that it must be treated as continuous, rather than discrete

Coulumb

The International System of Units (SI) unit of electric charge.

Coulomb force

another term for the electrostatic force

Coulomb's law

mathematical equation calculating the electrostatic force vector between two charged particles

dipole

two equal and opposite charges that are fixed close to each other

electric charge

physical property of an object that causes it to be attracted toward or repelled from another charged object; each charged object generates and is influenced by a force called an electric force

electric field

physical phenomenon created by a charge; it "transmits" a force between a two charges

electric force

noncontact force observed between electrically charged objects

electron

particle surrounding the nucleus of an atom and carrying the smallest unit of negative charge

Further Reading: Physics, High School by Urone, Paul Peter — openstax.org/details/books/physics
Creative Commons Attribution License v4.0

electrostatic attraction

phenomenon of two objects with opposite charges attracting each other

electrostatic force

amount and direction of attraction or repulsion between two charged bodies; the assumption is that the source charges have no acceleration

electrostatic repulsion

phenomenon of two objects with like charges repelling each other

electrostatics

study of charged objects which are not in motion

field line

smooth, usually curved line that indicates the direction of the electric field

field line density

number of field lines per square meter passing through an imaginary area; its purpose is to indicate the field strength at different points in space

induced dipole

typically an atom, or a spherically symmetric molecule; a dipole created due to opposite forces displacing the positive and negative charges

infinite plane

flat sheet in which the dimensions making up the area are much, much greater than its thickness, and also much, much greater than the distance at which the field is to be calculated; its field is constant

infinite straight wire

Further Reading: Physics, High School by Urone, Paul Peter — openstax.org/details/books/physics
Creative Commons Attribution License v4.0

straight wire whose length is much, much greater than either of its other dimensions, and also much, much greater than the distance at which the field is to be calculated

insulator

material that holds electrons securely within their atomic orbits

ion

atom or molecule with more or fewer electrons than protons

law of conservation of charge

net electric charge of a closed system is constant

linear charge density

amount of charge in an element of a charge distribution that is essentially one-dimensional (the width and height are much, much smaller than its length); its units are C/m

neutron

neutral particle in the nucleus of an atom, with (nearly) the same mass as a proton

permanent dipole

typically a molecule; a dipole created by the arrangement of the charged particles from which the dipole is created

permittivity of vacuum

also called the permittivity of free space, and constant describing the strength of the electric force in a vacuum

polarization

Further Reading: Physics, High School by Urone, Paul Peter — openstax.org/details/books/physics
Creative Commons Attribution License v4.0

slight shifting of positive and negative charges to opposite sides of an object

principle of superposition

useful fact that we can simply add up all of the forces due to charges acting on an object

proton

particle in the nucleus of an atom and carrying a positive charge equal in magnitude to the amount of negative charge carried by an electron

static electricity

buildup of electric charge on the surface of an object; the arrangement of the charge remains constant ("static")

superposition

concept that states that the net electric field of multiple source charges is the vector sum of the field of each source charge calculated individually

surface charge density

amount of charge in an element of a two-dimensional charge distribution (the thickness is small); its units are C/m^2 C/m^2

volume charge density

amount of charge in an element of a three-dimensional charge distribution; its units are C/m^3

Sample ASVAB questions

Here are some examples of the sort of questions you'll see on ASVAB subtests.

Remember, you have access to several full-length practice tests at ASVABcram.com.

Further Reading: Physics, High School by Urone, Paul Peter — openstax.org/details/books/physics
Creative Commons Attribution License v4.0

Electronics Information

1. The abbreviation BW stands for what?

a. Bandwidth

b. Beta Worth

c. Current Gain

d. Bi-voltage

(correct answer is a, Bandwidth)

2. What is the basic component of a light dimmer?

a. Diode

b. Transistor

c. Breadboard

d. Variable Resistor

(correct answer is d, Variable Resistor)

3. What is an LED?

a. Laser Equal Dot

b. Light Emitting Diode

c. Long Electronic Design

Further Reading: Physics, High School by Urone, Paul Peter — openstax.org/details/books/physics
Creative Commons Attribution License v4.0

d. Length Equalizer Diamond

(correct answer is b, Light Emitting Diode.)

4. Semiconductors are often made of what material?

a. Silicon

b. Sand

c. Copper

d. Rubber

(correct answer is a, Silicon.)

Further Reading: Physics, High School by Urone, Paul Peter — openstax.org/details/books/physics
Creative Commons Attribution License v4.0

► ARITHMETIC REASONING & MATH

On the ASVAB, the Arithmetic Reasoning consists of 16 questions involving high school math requiring calculations. Along with the subtest on Mathematics knowledge, this area combines for roughly half of your all-important AFQT score.

Both of these subtests, Arithmetic and Math, and covered in this section of this book.

Many people get turned off from math early in their schooling. But the truth is, the analytical and problem-solving skills based on arithmetic are essential for everyday life, and they're easily absorbed. These skills are essential for a military career because they're the foundation for future learning.

Math knowledge can help advance any career, even those that you might not think are related to math at first glance.

Arithmetic reasoning

Here's a problem-solving strategy you can use:

Step 1. Read the word problem. Make sure you understand all the words and ideas. You may need to read the problem two or more times. If there are words you don't understand, look them up in a dictionary or on the internet.

Step 2. Identify what you are looking for.

Step 3. Name what you are looking for. Choose a variable to represent that quantity.

Step 4. Translate into an equation. It may be helpful to first restate the problem in one sentence before translating.

Step 5. Solve the equation using good algebra techniques.

Step 6. Check the answer in the problem. Make sure it makes sense.

Step 7. Answer the question with a complete sentence.

Now we'll review some of the building blocks for making our calculations.

Whole numbers

Algebra uses numbers and symbols to represent words and ideas. Let's look at the numbers first. The most basic numbers used in algebra are those we use to count objects: 1, 2, 3, 4, 5, ... and so on. These are called the counting numbers. The notation "..." is called an ellipsis, which is another way to show "and so on", or that the pattern continues endlessly. Counting numbers are also called natural numbers.

The counting numbers start with 1 and continue: 1,2,3,4,5...

Counting numbers and whole numbers can be visualized on a number line as:

The point labeled 0 is called the origin. The points are equally spaced to the right of 0 and labeled with the counting numbers. When a number is paired with a point, it is called the coordinate of the point.

Example:

Which of the following are ⓐ counting numbers? ⓑ whole numbers?

Further Reading: Math in Society by Lippman, David — opentextbookstore.com/mathinsociety
Creative Commons Attribution-ShareAlike 3.0
Pre-Algebra by Marecek, Lynn — openstax.org/details/books/prealgebra-2e
Creative Commons Attribution License v4.0

$$0, \frac{1}{4}, 3, 5.2, 15, 105$$

Answer:

ⓐ The counting numbers start at 1, so 0 is not a counting number. The numbers 3, 15, and 105 are all counting numbers.

ⓑ Whole numbers are counting numbers and 0. The numbers 0, 3, 15, and 105 are whole numbers.

The numbers 1/4 and 5.2 are neither counting numbers nor whole numbers. We will discuss these numbers later.

Model Whole Numbers

Our number system is called a **place value system** because the value of a digit depends on its position, or place, in a number. The number 537 has a different value than the number 735. Even though they use the same digits, their value is different because of the different placement of the 3 and the 7 and the 5.

Three $100 bills	Seven $10 bills	Four $1 bills
3 × $100	7 × $10	4 × $1
$300	$70	$4

Money gives us a familiar model of place value. Suppose a wallet contains three $100 bills, seven $10 bills, and four $1 bills. The amounts are summarized in Figure 1.3. How much money is in the wallet?

Further Reading: Math in Society by Lippman, David — opentextbookstore.com/mathinsociety
Creative Commons Attribution-ShareAlike 3.0
Pre-Algebra by Marecek, Lynn — openstax.org/details/books/prealgebra-2e
Creative Commons Attribution License v4.0

Find the total value of each kind of bill, and then add to find the total. The wallet contains $374.

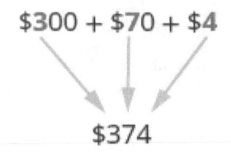

Round Whole Numbers

Recently the U.S. Census Bureau reported the population of New York state as 19,651,127 people. It might be enough to say that the population is approximately 20 million. The word approximately means that 20 million is not the exact population, but is close to the exact value.

The process of approximating a number is called rounding. Numbers are rounded to a specific place value depending on how much accuracy is needed. 20 million was achieved by rounding to the millions place. Had we rounded to the one hundred thousands place, we would have 19,700,000 as a result. Had we rounded to the ten thousands place, we would have 19,650,000 as a result, and so on. The place value to which we round to depends on how we need to use the number.

Using the number line can help you visualize and understand the rounding process. Look at the number line in Figure 1.7. Suppose we want to round the number 76 to the nearest ten. Is 76 closer to 70 or 80 on the number line?

We can see that 76 is closer to 80 than to 70. So 76 rounded to the nearest ten is 80.

So that everyone rounds the same way when a number is midway between the nearest tens, mathematicians have agreed to round to the higher number. So, 75 rounded to the nearest ten is 80.

Example:

Round 147,032 to the nearest thousand.

Answer:

Locate the thousands place. Underline the digit to the right of the thousands place.

The digit to the right of the thousands place is 0. Since 0 is less than 5, we do not change the digit in the thousands place.

We then replace all digits to the right of the thousands pace with zeros: 147,000.

Key terms

Let's review some key terminology:

Coordinate: A number paired with a point on a number line is called the coordinate of the point.

Counting numbers: The counting numbers are the numbers 1, 2, 3, ….

Difference: The difference is the result of subtracting two or more numbers.

Dividend: When dividing two numbers, the dividend is the number being divided.

Further Reading: Math in Society by Lippman, David — opentextbookstore.com/mathinsociety
Creative Commons Attribution-ShareAlike 3.0
Pre-Algebra by Marecek, Lynn — openstax.org/details/books/prealgebra-2e
Creative Commons Attribution License v4.0

Divisor: When dividing two numbers, the divisor is the number dividing the dividend.

Number line: A number line is used to visualize numbers. The numbers on the number line get larger as they go from left to right, and smaller as they go from right to left.

Origin: The origin is the point labeled 0 on a number line.

Place value system: Our number system is called a place value system because the value of a digit depends on its position, or place, in a number.

Product: The product is the result of multiplying two or more numbers.

Quotient: The quotient is the result of dividing two numbers.

Rounding: The process of approximating a number is called rounding.

Sum: The sum is the result of adding two or more numbers.

Whole numbers: The whole numbers are the numbers 0, 1, 2, 3, ….

Using the language of algebra

Using variables and algebraic symbols

Greg and Alex have the same birthday, but they were born in different years. This year Greg is 20 years old and Alex is 23, so Alex is 3 years older than Greg. When Greg was 12, Alex was 15. When Greg is 35, Alex will be 38. No matter what Greg's age is, Alex's age will always be 3 years more, right?

In the language of algebra, we say that Greg's age and Alex's age are variable and the three is a constant. The ages change, or vary, so age is a variable. The 3 years between them always stays the same, so the age difference is the constant.

In algebra, letters of the alphabet are used to represent variables. Suppose we call Greg's age g. Then we could use g+3 to represent Alex's age.

Further Reading: Math in Society by Lippman, David — opentextbookstore.com/mathinsociety
Creative Commons Attribution-ShareAlike 3.0
Pre-Algebra by Marecek, Lynn — openstax.org/details/books/prealgebra-2e
Creative Commons Attribution License v4.0

Greg's age	Alex's age
12	15
20	23
35	38
g	$g + 3$

Letters are used to represent variables, which may change. Letters often used for variables are x, y, a, b, and c. A constant is a number whose value always stays the same.

To write algebraically, we need some symbols as well as numbers and variables. There are several types of symbols we will be using. In Whole Numbers, we introduced the symbols for the four basic arithmetic operations: addition, subtraction, multiplication, and division. We will summarize them here, along with words we use for the operations and the result.

Operation	Notation	Say:	The result is...
Addition	$a + b$	a plus b	the sum of a and b
Subtraction	$a - b$	a minus b	the difference of a and b
Multiplication	$a \cdot b, (a)(b), (a)b, a(b)$	a times b	The product of a and b
Division	$a \div b, a/b, \frac{a}{b}, b\overline{)a}$	a divided by b	The quotient of a and b

Simplifying expressions with exponents

To simplify a numerical expression means to do all the math possible. For example, to simplify 4·2+1 we'd first multiply 4·2 to get 8 and then add the 1 to

Further Reading: Math in Society by Lippman, David — opentextbookstore.com/mathinsociety
Creative Commons Attribution-ShareAlike 3.0
Pre-Algebra by Marecek, Lynn — openstax.org/details/books/prealgebra-2e
Creative Commons Attribution License v4.0

get 9. A good habit to develop is to work down the page, writing each step of the process below the previous step.

Suppose we have the expression $2 \cdot 2 \cdot 2 \cdot 2 \cdot 2 \cdot 2 \cdot 2 \cdot 2 \cdot 2$. We could write this more compactly using exponential notation. Exponential notation is used in algebra to represent a quantity multiplied by itself several times. We write $2 \cdot 2 \cdot 2$ as 2^3 and $2 \cdot 2 \cdot 2 \cdot 2 \cdot 2 \cdot 2 \cdot 2 \cdot 2 \cdot 2$ as 2^9. In expressions such as 2^3, the 2 is called the base and the 3 is called the exponent. The exponent tells us how many factors of the base we have to multiply.

Exponential Notation	In Words
7^2	7 to the second power, or 7 squared
5^3	5 to the third power, or 5 cubed
9^4	9 to the fourth power
12^5	12 to the fifth power

Simplifying expressions using the order of operations

We've introduced most of the symbols and notation used in algebra, but now we need to clarify the order of operations. Otherwise, expressions may have different meanings, and they may result in different values.

For example, consider the expression:

$$4 + 3 \cdot 7$$

Some students say it simplifies to 49.

	$4 + 3 \cdot 7$
Since $4 + 3$ gives 7.	$7 \cdot 7$
And $7 \cdot 7$ is 49.	49

Some students say it simplifies to 25.

	$4 + 3 \cdot 7$
Since $3 \cdot 7$ is 21.	$4 + 21$
And $21 + 4$ makes 25.	25

Further Reading: Math in Society by Lippman, David — opentextbookstore.com/mathinsociety
Creative Commons Attribution-ShareAlike 3.0
Pre-Algebra by Marecek, Lynn — openstax.org/details/books/prealgebra-2e
Creative Commons Attribution License v4.0

Imagine the confusion that could result if every problem had several different correct answers. The same expression should give the same result. So mathematicians established some guidelines called the order of operations, which outlines the order in which parts of an expression must be simplified.

Order of operations

When simplifying mathematical expressions perform the operations in the following order:

1. Parentheses and other Grouping Symbols

Simplify all expressions inside the parentheses or other grouping symbols, working on the innermost parentheses first.

2. Exponents

Simplify all expressions with exponents.

3. Multiplication and Division

Perform all multiplication and division in order from left to right. These operations have equal priority.

4. Addition and Subtraction

Perform all addition and subtraction in order from left to right. These operations have equal priority.

Further Reading: Math in Society by Lippman, David — opentextbookstore.com/mathinsociety
Creative Commons Attribution-ShareAlike 3.0
Pre-Algebra by Marecek, Lynn — openstax.org/details/books/prealgebra-2e
Creative Commons Attribution License v4.0

Order of Operations	
Please	**P**arentheses
Excuse	**E**xponents
My **D**ear	**M**ultiplication and **D**ivision
Aunt **S**ally	**A**ddition and **S**ubtraction

Example:

Simplify:

ⓐ $18 \div 9 \cdot 2$

ⓑ $18 \cdot 9 \div 2$

Answer:

Further Reading: Math in Society by Lippman, David — opentextbookstore.com/mathinsociety
Creative Commons Attribution-ShareAlike 3.0
Pre-Algebra by Marecek, Lynn — openstax.org/details/books/prealgebra-2e
Creative Commons Attribution License v4.0

ⓐ	
	$18 \div 9 \cdot 2$
Are there any **p**arentheses? No.	
Are there any **e**xponents? No.	
Is there any **m**ultiplication or **d**ivision? Yes.	
Multiply and divide from left to right. Divide.	$2 \cdot 2$
Multiply.	4

ⓑ	
	$18 \cdot 9 \div 2$
Are there any **p**arentheses? No.	
Are there any **e**xponents? No.	
Is there any **m**ultiplication or **d**ivision? Yes.	
Multiply and divide from left to right.	
Multiply.	$162 \div 2$
Divide.	81

Example:

$2^3 - 12 \div (9-5)$

Answer:

5

Further Reading: Math in Society by Lippman, David — opentextbookstore.com/mathinsociety
Creative Commons Attribution-ShareAlike 3.0
Pre-Algebra by Marecek, Lynn — openstax.org/details/books/prealgebra-2e
Creative Commons Attribution License v4.0

Determining whether a number is a solution to an equation

Step 1. Substitute the number for the variable in the equation.

Step 2. Simplify the expressions on both sides of the equation.

Step 3. Determine whether the resulting equation is true.

If it is true, the number is a solution.

If it is not true, the number is not a solution.

Example:

Determine whether x=5 is a solution of 6x−17=16.

	$6x - 17 = 16$
Substitute 5 for x.	$6 \cdot 5 - 17 \overset{?}{=} 16$
Multiply.	$30 - 17 \overset{?}{=} 16$
Subtract.	$13 \neq 16$

So $x = 5$ is not a solution to the equation $6x - 17 = 16$.

Fractions

In working with equivalent fractions, you saw that there are many ways to write fractions that have the same value, or represent the same part of the whole. How do you know which one to use? Often, we'll use the fraction that is in simplified form.

Further Reading: Math in Society by Lippman, David — opentextbookstore.com/mathinsociety
Creative Commons Attribution-ShareAlike 3.0
Pre-Algebra by Marecek, Lynn — openstax.org/details/books/prealgebra-2e
Creative Commons Attribution License v4.0

A fraction is considered simplified if there are no common factors, other than 1, in the numerator and denominator. If a fraction does have common factors in the numerator and denominator, we can reduce the fraction to its simplified form by removing the common factors.

Simplifying fractions

A fraction is considered simplified if there are no common factors in the numerator and denominator. Example:

- $\frac{2}{3}$ is simplified because there are no common factors of 2 and 3.

- $\frac{10}{15}$ is not simplified because 5 is a common factor of 10 and 15.

The process of simplifying a fraction is often called reducing the fraction. In the previous section, we used the Equivalent Fractions Property to find equivalent fractions. We can also use the Equivalent Fractions Property in reverse to simplify fractions. We rewrite the property to show both forms together.

Equivalent Fractions Property

If a, b, c are numbers where $b \neq 0$, $c \neq 0$, then

$$\frac{a}{b} = \frac{a \cdot c}{b \cdot c} \quad \text{and} \quad \frac{a \cdot c}{b \cdot c} = \frac{a}{b}.$$

Simplify a fraction.

Step 1. Rewrite the numerator and denominator to show the common factors. If needed, factor the numerator and denominator into prime numbers.

Step 2. Simplify, using the equivalent fractions property, by removing common factors.

Further Reading: Math in Society by Lippman, David — opentextbookstore.com/mathinsociety
Creative Commons Attribution-ShareAlike 3.0
Pre-Algebra by Marecek, Lynn — openstax.org/details/books/prealgebra-2e
Creative Commons Attribution License v4.0

Step 3. Multiply any remaining factors.

Example:

Simplify: $\dfrac{5xy}{15x}$.	
⊘ **Solution**	
	$\dfrac{5xy}{15x}$
Rewrite numerator and denominator showing common factors.	$\dfrac{5 \cdot x \cdot y}{3 \cdot 5 \cdot x}$
Remove common factors.	$\dfrac{\cancel{5} \cdot \cancel{x} \cdot y}{3 \cdot \cancel{5} \cdot \cancel{x}}$
Simplify.	$\dfrac{y}{3}$

Multiplying fractions

Example:

Use a diagram to model $\dfrac{1}{2} \cdot \dfrac{3}{4}$.

⊘ **Solution**

First shade in $\dfrac{3}{4}$ of the rectangle.

We will take $\dfrac{1}{2}$ of this $\dfrac{3}{4}$, so we heavily shade $\dfrac{1}{2}$ of the shaded region.

Notice that 3 out of the 8 pieces are heavily shaded. This means that $\dfrac{3}{8}$ of the rectangle is heavily shaded.

Therefore, $\dfrac{1}{2}$ of $\dfrac{3}{4}$ is $\dfrac{3}{8}$, or $\dfrac{1}{2} \cdot \dfrac{3}{4} = \dfrac{3}{8}$.

Identifying and using fraction operations

Further Reading: Math in Society by Lippman, David — opentextbookstore.com/mathinsociety
Creative Commons Attribution-ShareAlike 3.0
Pre-Algebra by Marecek, Lynn — openstax.org/details/books/prealgebra-2e
Creative Commons Attribution License v4.0

You need a common denominator to add or subtract fractions, but not to multiply or divide fractions.

Summary of Fraction Operations

Fraction multiplication: Multiply the numerators and multiply the denominators.

$$\frac{a}{b} \cdot \frac{c}{d} = \frac{ac}{bd}$$

Fraction division: Multiply the first fraction by the reciprocal of the second.

$$\frac{a}{b} \div \frac{c}{d} = \frac{a}{b} \cdot \frac{d}{c}$$

Fraction addition: Add the numerators and place the sum over the common denominator. If the fractions have different denominators, first convert them to equivalent forms with the LCD.

$$\frac{a}{c} + \frac{b}{c} = \frac{a+b}{c}$$

Fraction subtraction: Subtract the numerators and place the difference over the common denominator. If the fractions have different denominators, first convert them to equivalent forms with the LCD.

$$\frac{a}{c} - \frac{b}{c} = \frac{a-b}{c}$$

Decimals

You probably already know quite a bit about decimals based on your experience with money. Suppose you buy a sandwich and a bottle of water for lunch. If the sandwich costs $3.45 , the bottle of water costs $1.25 , and the total sales tax is $0.33 , what is the total cost of your lunch?

$3.45	Sandwich
$1.25	Water
+ $0.33	Tax
$5.03	Total

When we name a whole number, the name corresponds to the place value based on the powers of ten. In Whole Numbers, we learned to read 10,000 as ten thousand. Likewise, the names of the decimal places correspond to their fraction values. Notice how the place value names in the table below relate to the names of the fractions.

Further Reading: Math in Society by Lippman, David — opentextbookstore.com/mathinsociety
Creative Commons Attribution-ShareAlike 3.0
Pre-Algebra by Marecek, Lynn — openstax.org/details/books/prealgebra-2e
Creative Commons Attribution License v4.0

Place Value											
Hundred thousands	Ten thousands	Thousands	Hundreds	Tens	Ones		Tenths	Hundredths	Thousandths	Ten-thousandths	Hundred-thousandths
						.					

Decimal operations

Example:

Subtract: 20–14.65.

	$20 - 14.65$
Write the numbers vertically so the decimal points line up. Remember 20 is a whole number, so place the decimal point after the 0.	20. − 14.65
Place two zeros after the decimal point in 20, as place holders so that both numbers have two decimal places.	20.00 − 14.65
Subtract the numbers as if they were whole numbers. Then place the decimal in the answer under the decimal points in the given numbers.	2̸0̸.0̸0̸ − 1 4 . 6 5 5 . 3 5

Multiplying decimals

Multiplying decimals is very much like multiplying whole numbers—we just have to determine where to place the decimal point. The procedure for multiplying decimals will make sense if we first review multiplying fractions.

Do you remember how to multiply fractions? To multiply fractions, you multiply the numerators and then multiply the denominators.

So let's see what we would get as the product of decimals by converting them to fractions first. We will do two examples side-by-side. Look for a pattern:

	A	B
	$(0.3)(0.7)$	$(0.2)(0.46)$
Convert to fractions.	$\left(\frac{3}{10}\right)\left(\frac{7}{10}\right)$	$\left(\frac{2}{10}\right)\left(\frac{46}{100}\right)$
Multiply.	$\frac{21}{100}$	$\frac{92}{1000}$
Convert back to decimals.	0.21	0.092

Solving equations with decimals

Now that we've worked with decimals, we are ready to find solutions to equations involving decimals. The steps we take to determine whether a number is a solution to an equation are the same whether the solution is a whole number, an integer, a fraction, or a decimal. We'll list these steps here again for easy reference.

HOW TO :: DETERMINE WHETHER A NUMBER IS A SOLUTION TO AN EQUATION.

Step 1.   Substitute the number for the variable in the equation.
Step 2.   Simplify the expressions on both sides of the equation.
Step 3.   Determine whether the resulting equation is true.
   ◦ If so, the number is a solution.
   ◦ If not, the number is not a solution.

Example:

Determine whether each of the following is a solution of $x - 0.7 = 1.5$:

Further Reading: Math in Society by Lippman, David — opentextbookstore.com/mathinsociety
Creative Commons Attribution-ShareAlike 3.0
Pre-Algebra by Marecek, Lynn — openstax.org/details/books/prealgebra-2e
Creative Commons Attribution License v4.0

ⓐ x=1

ⓑ x=−0.8

ⓒ x=2.2

Answer:

ⓐ

$$x - 0.7 = 1.5$$

Substitute 1 for x.	$1 - 0.7 \overset{?}{=} 1.5$
Subtract.	$0.3 \neq 1.5$

Since $x = 1$ does not result in a true equation, 1 is not a solution to the equation.

ⓑ

$$x - 0.7 = 1.5$$

Substitute −0.8 for x.	$-0.8 - 0.7 \overset{?}{=} 1.5$
Subtract.	$-1.5 \neq 1.5$

Since $x = -0.8$ does not result in a true equation, -0.8 is not a solution to the equation.

ⓒ

$$x - 0.7 = 1.5$$

Substitute 2.2 for x.	$2.2 - 0.7 \overset{?}{=} 1.5$
Subtract.	$1.5 = 1.5 \checkmark$

Since $x = 2.2$ results in a true equation, 2.2 is a solution to the equation.

Simplifying expressions with square roots

To start this section, we need to review some important vocabulary and notation. Remember that when a number n is multiplied by itself, we can write

Further Reading: Math in Society by Lippman, David — opentextbookstore.com/mathinsociety
Creative Commons Attribution-ShareAlike 3.0
Pre-Algebra by Marecek, Lynn — openstax.org/details/books/prealgebra-2e
Creative Commons Attribution License v4.0

this as n^2, which we read aloud as "n squared." For example, 8^2 is read as "8 squared."

We call 64 the *square* of 8 because $8^2=64$. Similarly, 121 is the square of 11, because $11^2=121$.

If $n^2=m$, then m is the square of n.

Square root of a number

A number whose square is m is called a square root of m.

If $n^2=m$, then n is a square root of m.

Notice $(-10)^2=100$ also, so -10 is also a square root of 100. Therefore, both 10 and -10 are square roots of 100.

So, every positive number has two square roots: one positive and one negative.

What if we only want the positive square root of a positive number? The radical sign, $\sqrt{}$, stands for the positive square root. The positive square root is also called the **principal square root**.

Square root notation

$m--\sqrt{}$ is read as "the square root of m."

If $m=n^2$, then $\sqrt{m}=n$ for $n \geq 0$.

Percentages

In the 2004 vice-presidential debates, John Edwards claimed that US forces have suffered "90% of the coalition casualties" in Iraq. Dick Cheney disputed this, saying that in fact Iraqi security forces and coalition allies "have taken almost 50

Further Reading: Math in Society by Lippman, David — opentextbookstore.com/mathinsociety
Creative Commons Attribution-ShareAlike 3.0
Pre-Algebra by Marecek, Lynn — openstax.org/details/books/prealgebra-2e
Creative Commons Attribution License v4.0

percent" of the casualties. Who was correct? How can we make sense of these numbers?

Percent literally means "per 100," or "parts per hundred." When we write 40%, this is equivalent to the fraction $\dfrac{40}{100}$ or the decimal 0.40. Notice that 80 out of 200 and 10 out of 25 are also 40%, since $\dfrac{80}{200} = \dfrac{10}{25} = \dfrac{40}{100}$.

Example:

243 people out of 400 state that they like dogs. What percent is this?

$\dfrac{243}{400} = 0.6075 = \dfrac{60.75}{100}$. This is 60.75%.

Notice that the percent can be found from the equivalent decimal by moving the decimal point two places to the right.

Example:

Write each as a percent: a) $\dfrac{1}{4}$ b) 0.02 c) 2.35

a) $\dfrac{1}{4} = 0.25$ = 25%   b) 0.02 = 2%   c) 2.35 = 235%

a) $\dfrac{1}{4} = 0.25$ = 25%   b) 0.02 = 2%   c) 2.35 = 235%

Further Reading: Math in Society by Lippman, David — opentextbookstore.com/mathinsociety
Creative Commons Attribution-ShareAlike 3.0
Pre-Algebra by Marecek, Lynn — openstax.org/details/books/prealgebra-2e
Creative Commons Attribution License v4.0

> **Percents**
> If we have a *part* that is some *percent* of a *whole*, then
>
> $$\text{percent} = \frac{\text{part}}{\text{whole}}, \text{ or equivalently, } \text{part} = \text{percent} \cdot \text{whole}$$
>
> To do the calculations, we write the percent as a decimal.

The base of a percent is very important. For example, while Nixon was president, it was argued that marijuana was a "gateway" drug, claiming that 80% of marijuana smokers went on to use harder drugs like cocaine. The problem is, this isn't true. The true claim is that 80% of harder drug users first smoked marijuana. The difference is one of base: 80% of marijuana smokers using hard drugs, vs. 80% of hard drug users having smoked marijuana. These numbers are not equivalent. As it turns out, only one in 2,400 marijuana users actually go on to use harder drugs.

> **Absolute and Relative Change**
> Given two quantities,
>
> Absolute change = |ending quantity − starting quantity|
>
> Relative change: $\dfrac{\text{absolute change}}{\text{starting quantity}}$
>
> Absolute change has the same units as the original quantity.
> Relative change gives a percent change.
> The starting quantity is called the **base** of the percent change.

Example:

There are about 75 QFC supermarkets in the U.S. Albertsons has about 215 stores. Compare the size of the two companies.

When we make comparisons, we must ask first whether an absolute or relative comparison. The absolute difference is 215 − 75 = 140. From this, we could say "Albertsons has 140 more stores than QFC." However, if you wrote this in an article or paper, that number does not mean much. The relative difference may be

Further Reading: Math in Society by Lippman, David — opentextbookstore.com/mathinsociety
Creative Commons Attribution-ShareAlike 3.0
Pre-Algebra by Marecek, Lynn — openstax.org/details/books/prealgebra-2e
Creative Commons Attribution License v4.0

more meaningful. There are two different relative changes we could calculate, depending on which store we use as the base:

Using QFC as the base, $\frac{140}{75} = 1.867$.

This tells us Albertsons is 186.7% larger than QFC.

Using Albertsons as the base, $\frac{140}{215} = 0.651$.

This tells us QFC is 65.1% smaller than Albertsons.

Notice both of these are showing percent *differences*. We could also calculate the size of Albertsons relative to QFC: $\frac{215}{75} = 2.867$, which tells us Albertsons is 2.867 times the size of QFC. Likewise, we could calculate the size of QFC relative to Albertsons: $\frac{75}{215} = 0.349$, which tells us that QFC is 34.9% of the size of Albertsons.

Proportions and Rates

If you wanted to power the city of Seattle using wind power, how many windmills would you need to install? Questions like these can be answered using rates and proportions.

Rates
A rate is the ratio (fraction) of two quantities.
A **unit rate** is a rate with a denominator of one.

Example:

Your car can drive 300 miles on a tank of 15 gallons. Express this as a rate.

Expressed as a rate, $\frac{300\,\text{miles}}{15\,\text{gallons}}$. We can divide to find a unit rate: $\frac{20\,\text{miles}}{1\,\text{gallon}}$, which we could also write as $20\frac{\text{miles}}{\text{gallon}}$, or just 20 miles per gallon.

Further Reading: Math in Society by Lippman, David — opentextbookstore.com/mathinsociety
Creative Commons Attribution-ShareAlike 3.0
Pre-Algebra by Marecek, Lynn — openstax.org/details/books/prealgebra-2e
Creative Commons Attribution License v4.0

> **Proportion Equation**
> A proportion equation is an equation showing the equivalence of two rates or ratios.

Example:

Solve the proportion $\dfrac{5}{3} = \dfrac{x}{6}$ for the unknown value x.

This proportion is asking us to find a fraction with denominator 6 that is equivalent to the fraction $\dfrac{5}{3}$. We can solve this by multiplying both sides of the equation by 6, giving

$$x = \frac{5}{3} \cdot 6 = 10.$$

Example:

A map scale indicates that ½ inch on the map corresponds with 3 real miles. How many miles apart are two cities that are $2\dfrac{1}{4}$ inches apart on the map?

We can set up a proportion by setting equal two $\dfrac{\text{map inches}}{\text{real miles}}$ rates, and introducing a variable, x, to represent the unknown quantity – the mile distance between the cities.

$$\frac{\frac{1}{2}\,\text{map inch}}{3\,\text{miles}} = \frac{2\frac{1}{4}\,\text{map inches}}{x\,\text{miles}}$$

Multiply both sides by x
and rewriting the mixed number

$$\frac{\frac{1}{2}}{3} \cdot x = \frac{9}{4}$$

Multiply both sides by 3

$$\frac{1}{2}x = \frac{27}{4}$$

Multiply both sides by 2 (or divide by ½)

$$x = \frac{27}{2} = 13\frac{1}{2}\ \text{miles}$$

Dimensional analysis can also be used to do unit conversions. Here are some unit conversions for reference.

Unit Conversions
Length
1 foot (ft) = 12 inches (in)   1 yard (yd) = 3 feet (ft)
1 mile = 5,280 feet
1000 millimeters (mm) = 1 meter (m)   100 centimeters (cm) = 1 meter
1000 meters (m) = 1 kilometer (km)   2.54 centimeters (cm) = 1 inch

Weight and Mass
1 pound (lb) = 16 ounces (oz)   1 ton = 2000 pounds
1000 milligrams (mg) = 1 gram (g)   1000 grams = 1kilogram (kg)
1 kilogram = 2.2 pounds (on earth)

Capacity
1 cup = 8 fluid ounces (fl oz)[*]   1 pint = 2 cups
1 quart = 2 pints = 4 cups   1 gallon = 4 quarts = 16 cups
1000 milliliters (ml) = 1 liter (L)

[*]Fluid ounces are a capacity measurement for liquids. 1 fluid ounce $\approx$ 1 ounce (weight) for water only.

Example:

A bicycle is traveling at 15 miles per hour. How many feet will it cover in 20 seconds?

To answer this question, we need to convert 20 seconds into feet. If we know the speed of the bicycle in feet per second, this question would be simpler. Since we don't, we will need to do additional unit conversions. We will need to know that 5280 ft = 1 mile. We might start by converting the 20 seconds into hours:

$$20\,\text{seconds} \cdot \frac{1\,\text{minute}}{60\,\text{seconds}} \cdot \frac{1\,\text{hour}}{60\,\text{minutes}} = \frac{1}{180}\,\text{hour}$$ Now we can multiply by the 15 miles/hr

$$\frac{1}{180}\,\text{hour} \cdot \frac{15\,\text{miles}}{1\,\text{hour}} = \frac{1}{12}\,\text{mile}$$ Now we can convert to feet

$$\frac{1}{12}\,\text{mile} \cdot \frac{5280\,\text{feet}}{1\,\text{mile}} = 440\,\text{feet}$$

We could have also done this entire calculation in one long set of products:

$$20\,\text{seconds} \cdot \frac{1\,\text{minute}}{60\,\text{seconds}} \cdot \frac{1\,\text{hour}}{60\,\text{minutes}} \cdot \frac{15\,\text{miles}}{1\,\text{hour}} \cdot \frac{5280\,\text{feet}}{1\,\text{mile}} = 440\,\text{feet}$$

Further Reading: Math in Society by Lippman, David — opentextbookstore.com/mathinsociety
Creative Commons Attribution-ShareAlike 3.0
Pre-Algebra by Marecek, Lynn — openstax.org/details/books/prealgebra-2e
Creative Commons Attribution License v4.0

Geometry

Geometric shapes, as well as area and volumes, can often be important in problem solving. It may be helpful to recall some formulas for areas and volumes of a few basic shapes.

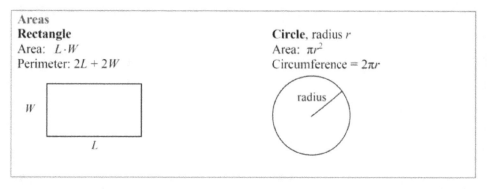

Areas
Rectangle
Area: $L \cdot W$
Perimeter: $2L + 2W$

Circle, radius r
Area: πr^2
Circumference $= 2\pi r$

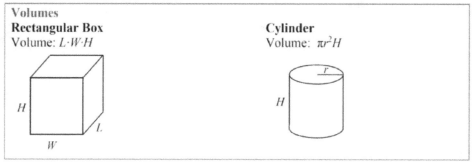

Volumes
Rectangular Box
Volume: $L \cdot W \cdot H$

Cylinder
Volume: $\pi r^2 H$

Geometric formulas

Dimensions:

Further Reading: Math in Society by Lippman, David — opentextbookstore.com/mathinsociety
Creative Commons Attribution-ShareAlike 3.0
Pre-Algebra by Marecek, Lynn — openstax.org/details/books/prealgebra-2e
Creative Commons Attribution License v4.0

Name	Shape	Formulas
Rectangle		Perimeter: $P = 2l + 2w$ Area: $A = lw$
Square		Perimeter: $P = 4s$ Area: $A = s^2$
Triangle		Perimeter: $P = a + b + c$ Area: $A = \frac{1}{2}bh$ Sum of Angles: $A + B + C = 180°$
Right Triangle		Pythagorean Theorem: $a^2 + b^2 = c^2$ Area: $A = \frac{1}{2}ab$
Circle		Circumference: $C = 2\pi r$ or $C = \pi d$ Area: $A = \pi r^2$
Parellelogram		Perimeter: $P = 2a + 2b$ Area: $A = bh$
Trapezoid		Perimeter: $P = a + b + c + B$ Area: $A = \frac{1}{2}(B + b)h$

Further Reading: Math in Society by Lippman, David — opentextbookstore.com/mathinsociety
Creative Commons Attribution-ShareAlike 3.0
Pre-Algebra by Marecek, Lynn — openstax.org/details/books/prealgebra-2e
Creative Commons Attribution License v4.0

Example:

If a 12 inch diameter pizza requires 10 ounces of dough, how much dough is needed for a 16 inch pizza?

To answer this question, we need to consider how the weight of the dough will scale. The weight will be based on the volume of the dough. However, since both pizzas will be about the same thickness, the weight will scale with the area of the top of the pizza. We can find the area of each pizza using the formula for area of a circle, $A = \pi r^2$:

A 12" pizza has radius 6 inches, so the area will be $\pi 6^2$ = about 113 square inches.
A 16" pizza has radius 8 inches, so the area will be $\pi 8^2$ = about 201 square inches.

Notice that if both pizzas were 1 inch thick, the volumes would be 113 in^3 and 201 in^3 respectively, which are at the same ratio as the areas. As mentioned earlier, since the thickness is the same for both pizzas, we can safely ignore it.

We can now set up a proportion to find the weight of the dough for a 16" pizza:

$$\frac{10\,\text{ounces}}{113\,\text{in}^2} = \frac{x\,\text{ounces}}{201\,\text{in}^2}$$ Multiply both sides by 201

$$x = 201 \cdot \frac{10}{113} = \text{about 17.8 ounces of dough for a 16" pizza.}$$

Problem Solving and Estimating

Now we will bring together the mathematical tools we've reviewed, and use them to approach more complex problems. In many problems, it is tempting to take the given information, plug it into whatever formulas you have handy, and hope that the result is what you were supposed to find. Chances are, this approach has served you well in other math classes.

This approach does not work well with real life problems. Instead, problem solving is best approached by first starting at the end: identifying exactly what you are looking for. From there, you then work backwards, asking "what information and procedures will I need to find this?" Very few interesting questions can be answered in one mathematical step; often times you will need to chain together a solution pathway, a series of steps that will allow you to answer the question.

Further Reading: Math in Society by Lippman, David — opentextbookstore.com/mathinsociety
Creative Commons Attribution-ShareAlike 3.0
Pre-Algebra by Marecek, Lynn — openstax.org/details/books/prealgebra-2e
Creative Commons Attribution License v4.0

> **Problem Solving Process**
> 1. Identify the question you're trying to answer.
> 2. Work backwards, identifying the information you will need and the relationships you will use to answer that question.
> 3. Continue working backwards, creating a solution pathway.
> 4. If you are missing necessary information, look it up or estimate it. If you have unnecessary information, ignore it.
> 5. Solve the problem, following your solution pathway.

In most problems we work, we will be approximating a solution, because we will not have perfect information. We will begin with a few examples where we will be able to approximate the solution using basic knowledge from our lives.

Example:

How many times does your heart beat in a year?

This question is asking for the rate of heart beats per year. Since a year is a long time to measure heart beats for, if we knew the rate of heart beats per minute, we could scale that quantity up to a year. So the information we need to answer this question is heart beats per minute. This is something you can easily measure by counting your pulse while watching a clock for a minute.

Suppose you count 80 beats in a minute. To convert this beats per year:

$$\frac{80 \text{ beats}}{1 \text{ minute}} \cdot \frac{60 \text{ minutes}}{1 \text{ hour}} \cdot \frac{24 \text{ hours}}{1 \text{ day}} \cdot \frac{365 \text{ days}}{1 \text{ year}} = 42,048,000 \text{ beats per year}$$

A recipe for zucchini muffins states that it yields 12 muffins, with 250 calories per muffin. You instead decide to make mini-muffins, and the recipe yields 20 muffins. If you eat 4, how many calories will you consume?

There are several possible solution pathways to answer this question. We will explore one.

To answer the question of how many calories 4 mini-muffins will contain, we would want to know the number of calories in each mini-muffin. To find the calories in each mini-muffin, we could first find the total calories for the entire

Further Reading: Math in Society by Lippman, David — opentextbookstore.com/mathinsociety
Creative Commons Attribution-ShareAlike 3.0
Pre-Algebra by Marecek, Lynn — openstax.org/details/books/prealgebra-2e
Creative Commons Attribution License v4.0

ARITHMETIC REASONING & MATH | 189

recipe, then divide it by the number of mini-muffins produced. To find the total calories for the recipe, we could multiply the calories per standard muffin by the number per muffin. Notice that this produces a multi-step solution pathway. It is often easier to solve a problem in small steps, rather than trying to find a way to jump directly from the given information to the solution.

We can now execute our plan:

$$12 \text{ muffins} \cdot \frac{250 \text{ calories}}{\text{muffin}} = 3000 \text{ calories for the whole recipe}$$

$$\frac{3000 \text{ calories}}{20 \text{ mini} - \text{muffins}} \text{ gives } 150 \text{ calories per mini-muffin}$$

$$4 \text{ mini muffins} \cdot \frac{150 \text{ calories}}{\text{mini} - \text{muffin}} \text{ totals } 600 \text{ calories consumed.}$$

Statistics

To properly evaluate the data and claims that bombard you every day. If you cannot distinguish good from faulty reasoning, then you are vulnerable to manipulation and to decisions that are not in your best interest. Statistics provides tools that you need in order to react intelligently to information you hear or read. In this sense, Statistics is one of the most important things that you can study.

To be more specific, here are some claims that we have heard on several occasions. (We are not saying that each one of these claims is true!)

- 4 out of 5 dentists recommend Dentyne.

- Almost 85% of lung cancers in men and 45% in women are tobacco-related.

- Condoms are effective 94% of the time.

Further Reading: Math in Society by Lippman, David — opentextbookstore.com/mathinsociety
Creative Commons Attribution-ShareAlike 3.0
Pre-Algebra by Marecek, Lynn — openstax.org/details/books/prealgebra-2e
Creative Commons Attribution License v4.0

- Native Americans are significantly more likely to be hit crossing the streets than are people of other ethnicities.

- People tend to be more persuasive when they look others directly in the eye and speak loudly and quickly.

- Women make 75 cents to every dollar a man makes when they work the same job.

- A surprising new study shows that eating egg whites can increase one's life span.

- People predict that it is very unlikely there will ever be another baseball player with a batting average over 400.

- There is an 80% chance that in a room full of 30 people that at least two people will share the same birthday.

- 79.48% of all statistics are made up on the spot.

All of these claims are statistical in character. We suspect that some of them sound familiar; if not, we bet that you have heard other claims like them. Notice how diverse the examples are; they come from psychology, health, law, sports, business, etc. Indeed, data and data-interpretation show up in discourse from virtually every facet of contemporary life.

Statistics are often presented in an effort to add credibility to an argument or advice. You can see this by paying attention to television advertisements. Many of the numbers thrown about in this way do not represent careful statistical analysis. They can be misleading, and push you into decisions that you might find cause to regret. For these reasons, learning about statistics is a long step towards taking control of your life.

Further Reading: Math in Society by Lippman, David — opentextbookstore.com/mathinsociety
Creative Commons Attribution-ShareAlike 3.0
Pre-Algebra by Marecek, Lynn — openstax.org/details/books/prealgebra-2e
Creative Commons Attribution License v4.0

Populations and samples

Before we begin gathering and analyzing data we need to characterize the population we are studying. If we want to study the amount of money spent on textbooks by a typical first-year college student, our population might be all first-year students at your college. Or it might be:

- All first-year community college students in the state of Washington.

- All first-year students at public colleges and universities in the state of Washington.

- All first-year students at all colleges and universities in the state of Washington.

- All first-year students at all colleges and universities in the entire United States.

And so on.

Population
The **population** of a study is the group the collected data is intended to describe.

Example:

A newspaper website contains a poll asking people their opinion on a recent news article.

What is the population?

While the target (intended) population may have been all people, the real population of the survey is readers of the website.

If we were able to gather data on every member of our population, say the average (we will define "average" more carefully in a subsequent section) amount of money spent on textbooks by each first-year student at your college during the 2020-2021 academic year, the resulting number would be called a parameter.

> **Parameter**
> A **parameter** is a value (average, percentage, etc.) calculated using all the data from a population

We seldom see parameters, however, since surveying an entire population is usually very time-consuming and expensive, unless the population is very small or we already have the data collected.

> **Census**
> A survey of an entire population is called a **census**.

You are probably familiar with two common censuses: the official government Census that attempts to count the population of the U.S. every ten years, and voting, which asks the opinion of all eligible voters in a district. The first of these demonstrates one additional problem with a census: the difficulty in finding and getting participation from everyone in a large population, which can bias, or skew, the results.

There are occasionally times when a census is appropriate, usually when the population is fairly small. For example, if the manager of Starbucks wanted to know the average number of hours her employees worked last week, she should be able to pull up payroll records or ask each employee directly.

Since surveying an entire population is often impractical, we usually select a sample to study.

> **Sample**
> A **sample** is a smaller subset of the entire population, ideally one that is fairly representative of the whole population.

Further Reading: Math in Society by Lippman, David — opentextbookstore.com/mathinsociety
Creative Commons Attribution-ShareAlike 3.0
Pre-Algebra by Marecek, Lynn — openstax.org/details/books/prealgebra-2e
Creative Commons Attribution License v4.0

If we survey a sample, say 100 first-year students at your college, and find the average amount of money spent by these students on textbooks, the resulting number is called a statistic.

Statistic
A **statistic** is a value (average, percentage, etc.) calculated using the data from a sample.

Example:

A researcher wanted to know how citizens of Tacoma felt about a voter initiative. To study this, she goes to the Tacoma Mall and randomly selects 500 shoppers and asks them their opinion. 60% indicate they are supportive of the initiative. What is the sample and population? Is the 60% value a parameter or a statistic?

The sample is the 500 shoppers questioned. The population is less clear. While the intended population of this survey was Tacoma citizens, the effective population was mall shoppers. There is no reason to assume that the 500 shoppers questioned would be representative of all Tacoma citizens.

The 60% value was based on the sample, so it is a statistic.

Example:

A college reports that the average age of their students is 28 years old. Is this a statistic or a parameter?

This is a parameter, since the college would have access to data on all students (the population).

Categorizing data

Once we have gathered data, we might wish to classify it. Roughly speaking, data can be classified as categorical data or quantitative data.

Further Reading: Math in Society by Lippman, David — opentextbookstore.com/mathinsociety
Creative Commons Attribution-ShareAlike 3.0
Pre-Algebra by Marecek, Lynn — openstax.org/details/books/prealgebra-2e
Creative Commons Attribution License v4.0

> **Quantitative and categorical data**
> **Categorical (qualitative) data** are pieces of information that allow us to classify the objects under investigation into various categories.
>
> **Quantitative data** are responses that are numerical in nature and with which we can perform meaningful arithmetic calculations.

We might conduct a survey to determine the name of the favorite movie that each person in a math class saw in a movie theater.

When we conduct such a survey, the responses would look like: *Finding Nemo*, *The Hulk*, or *Terminator 3: Rise of the Machines*. We might count the number of people who give each answer, but the answers themselves do not have any numerical values: we cannot perform computations with an answer like "*Finding Nemo*." This would be categorical data.

Example:

A survey could ask the number of movies you have seen in a movie theater in the past 12 months (0, 1, 2, 3, 4, ...)

This would be quantitative data.

Sample ASVAB questions

Here are some examples of the sort of questions you'll see on ASVAB subtests.

Remember, you have access to several full-length practice tests at ASVABcram.com.

Arithmetic Reasoning

1. There are 20 students in Robert's class, and there are only 5 other classes in the school, each having 15 students. How many students does the school have?

a. 80

b. 200

Further Reading: Math in Society by Lippman, David — opentextbookstore.com/mathinsociety
Creative Commons Attribution-ShareAlike 3.0
Pre-Algebra by Marecek, Lynn — openstax.org/details/books/prealgebra-2e
Creative Commons Attribution License v4.0

c. 225

d. 95

2. Melons are on sale at 5 for $7. How much would you pay for 12 melons?

a. $16.80

b. $15

c. $19

d. $25

(the correct answer is a, $16.80.)

3. A train is traveling at 60 miles per hour. How long will the train have traveled in 40 minutes?

25 miles

65 miles

150 miles

d. 40 miles

(correct answer is d, 40 miles)

Further Reading: Math in Society by Lippman, David — opentextbookstore.com/mathinsociety
Creative Commons Attribution-ShareAlike 3.0
Pre-Algebra by Marecek, Lynn — openstax.org/details/books/prealgebra-2e
Creative Commons Attribution License v4.0

4. A basket contains 7 baseballs and 28 softballs. Expressed in the lowest terms, what is the ratio between the baseballs and softballs?

a. 1:28

b. 1:4

c. 2:28

d. 7 x 28

(correct answer is b, 1:4).

Mathematics Knowledge

1. The ratio 72 : 24 is the same as:

a. 5: 1

b. 3: 1

c. 12 : 36

d. 1 : 5

(correct answer is b, 3: 1.)

2. $x - 6 = 10$. What is x?

a. Y

b. 20

Further Reading: Math in Society by Lippman, David — opentextbookstore.com/mathinsociety
Creative Commons Attribution-ShareAlike 3.0
Pre-Algebra by Marecek, Lynn — openstax.org/details/books/prealgebra-2e
Creative Commons Attribution License v4.0

c. 12

d. 16

(correct answer is d, 16.)

3. Solve 468 ÷ 9

a. 52

b. 102

c. 74

d. 48

correct answer is a, 52).

4. Solve √84 + 16

a. 15

b. 10

c. 12

d. 8

(Correct answer is b, 10.)

Further Reading: Math in Society by Lippman, David — opentextbookstore.com/mathinsociety
Creative Commons Attribution-ShareAlike 3.0
Pre-Algebra by Marecek, Lynn — openstax.org/details/books/prealgebra-2e
Creative Commons Attribution License v4.0

► ASSEMBLING OBJECTS

Assembling Objects

Which illustration shows how the shapes in the left box will appear when they are fitted together?

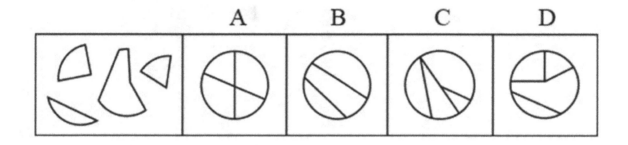

NOTE: This last subtest, Assembling Objects, is useful for only a small number of Navy enlistees intending to qualify for specific jobs. Because the subtest doesn't affect scoring for the vast majority of enlistees, it is not covered in this book.